EARLY MEDIEVAL STATE

(A STUDY OF DELHI SULTANATE)

Dr. L. S. Chandel

Commonwealth

EARLY MEDIEVAL STATE

Edition : 2025

ISBN 81-7169-011-4

Published by :
Commonwealth Publishers (P) Ltd.
4831/24, Govind Lane,
Ansari Road, Darya Ganj,
New Delhi - 110002
Ph. : 23272541, 23242541
e-mail : commonwealthpublishers2016@gmail.com

Distributed by :
Arjun Publishing House
4831/24, Govind Lane,
Ansari Road, Darya Ganj,
New Delhi - 110002
Ph. : 23272541, 23242541
e-mail : arjunbooks2001@gmail.com

Printed at :
Milan Enterprises
Delhi

PREFACE

The development of India is subject of absorbing interest and scholars are starting to pay attention to it. This interest is not merely arising act of the clashes of present day life in the India. We are studying the problems of workers, Judicial or racial conflicts during the past as well as in the present. The history of India which furnishes a striking illustration of the impact of many problems which are gradually transformed by a process of development. No doubtly, it requires the attention of a student of history who endeavours to understand the interactions of human-mind as well as the community and society.

In placing before the student of Indian History, I intends to bring my findings to their notice and study. It seeks to examine the aims and objectives of Sultans of Delhi towards the Hill Cheiftains of Present Himachal Pradesh particularly towards Sirmur and Nagarkot or Kangra.

India is primarily an agriculturist and Laboural country. The workers are formed the backbone of the country's economy. Slaves played a deciding role during the sultanate politics and Sultan patronised them. Where as the peasants and other professional-workers had to face the tyrannys of land lords, revenue officials, traders, hoarders and their masters. Although the produce of agriculture was the main source of state income and similarly the workers labour responsible for the increase in production.

Our variety personality Amir Khusrau was a world famous poet saint, musician, writer of the early medieval period, who had close-contact with sultans, nobles and Commoners. Wrote so many books in verses and in prose also. These works are full of the historical facts and knowledge as well as materials but he never assert himself a historian.

So many writers and historians asserted that Sultanate was a Theocratic-state but the works of Sultan, conditions of non-Muslims and 'Jaziya' arises the questions How—Were all the Sultans ruled for the Muslims, by the Muslims and to the Muslims ? I have to decide to re-examine the whole problem step by step. In this work I have selected one aspect, *i.e.*, "Nature of the Sultan's Campaigns", and trying to the re-examine the problem—Nature of state with the help of statistical datta and graph by applying the proportionate-method and concluded that facts speaks itself. I think this method of writing history is used for the first time.

Judicial administration is one of the most important pillars of the sound administration. Whereas, "Qazi" or Judge is the pivote of the judicial administration. Details about the role of "Qazi" during Sultanate is an important, to examine his position during the study period. Either he was free to decide according to the Cannon-Law or Shara or his decision were influenced by the contemporary Sultan's policy, nobles positions.

I am conscious about the inadequacy of the attempt or in other words, I do confess that I have not been able to do full justice to the subjects dealt with in this book. However, the lack of the authentic documents and other records at many places concluded at the analytical and open for correction or change when the datta available contradicting the conclusions.

It is my pleasant duty to express my very sincere and deep gratitude to my respected teacher. Dr. M.S. Ahluwalia (H.P. Univ., Shimla), Prof. Mohammad Aslm (Chairman of the History Department, Punjab University, Lahore), Prof. A.R. Khan (Head of the Department of History, H.P. University, Shimla) ; Dr. Dilbag Singh (J.N.U. New Delhi) for the encouragement, guidance as well as valuable suggestions. I once again express my sincere and deep gratitude to respected teacher Dr. M.S. Ahluwalia, and Prof. Moh. Aslm for going through the manuscript.

I also express my thanks to my wife Supreeti Chandel, the prolonged desire, *i.e.*, utilization of the whole material collected during my research period, would not have been completed even now but she showed patience and understanding during all this period of compiling and writing.

I also express my thanks to Principal G.R. Sharma (S.V.S.D. College, Bhatoli) who provides me opportunity to continue my research work. Thanks are also due to my colleagues in the (Previous) college, who are painfully going through the manuscript for language corrections and graphs explanations.

I also thanks to Mr. Anil Kumar, Inderjeet Sharma and Randhir Singh Katoch for their laborious task of typing.

Dr. L. S. Chandel

CONTENTS

1

*Military Campaigns in Early Medieval State**

All the contemporary and later chronicler of the Sultanate period have eulogised the Turkish Conquerors of Northern India as True Mussalmans and Campaigns of Islam. Their writings give an impression that the Sultan's every action and efforts was motivated by the religious beliefs and sentiments. They carried on a relentless *Jihad* to convert *Dar-ul-harb* into *Dar-ul-Islam* guided by such statements, a majority of modern writers too have attempted to portrait a similar picture. The exception is only the case of one or two modern writers who have not been misled by these assertions. Mohammed Habib for instance, has mentioned that the Turkish Sultans, "Undoubtedly were true Muslims but none of them was a True representative of Islam. Their actions were motivated mere by the wordly desires than by any religious motives".[1]

Conflicting views have been put forwarded by the modern writers as to whether the State in Early Medieval India was a theocracy or not. R.P. Tripathi unhesitatingly declares the medieval state as a theocracy.[2] Contrary to this I.H. Qureshi asserts that, "it is only the supermacy of *Shara* which has

*This paper is read in the 'Indian History Congress' held at Bombay, 1980.

confused the writers to declare the sultanate as a theocracy".[3] Qureshi's assertions however are open to certain doubts as he has tried to prove the medieval state as a secular in very embiguous terms.

In the introductory remarks to the *Fatawa-i-Jahandari*[4] of Ziauddin Barani, Mohd. Habib has categorically asserted that "It (the Sultanate of Delhi) was not a theocratic state in any sense of word. Its basis was not the *Shariat* of Islam but the *Zawabit* or state laws made by the King... It's foundation was nevertheless, non-religious and secular. It was not based on any religious texts or their interpretations by the *Ulama* but upon the opinion of the King (or the King and his advisers) as to what was good for the Kingdom and his people".[5]

Due to the conflicting views held by various writers it has become imperative to re-examine the whole issue on the basis of the historical events. An attempt is made here to study the various military campaigns of the Delhi Sultans. The whole problem have been attempted through a statistical and average proportionate method with a view to analyse the motives of the various campaigns. The study is also conducted with the help of graphs which indicate the percentage of the various campaigns led by Sultans against the Muslims and non-Muslims.[6]

Each Sultan had Muslim religious law (*Shariat*) as a model before him. Moreover, he was assisted by the *Ulama* and others who interpreted the religious text and gave the expert opinion.[7] However, with the exception of Sultan Ferozshah Tughluq rarely any of the sultans tried to govern the country on the basis of *Shariat* or strictly followed whatever, was dictated by the *Ulama*.[8] On the contrary many sultans were noted for their utter disregard of the Muslim Canon Law.[9]

The Sultans waged wars against both Muslims as well as Non-Muslims. Who ever disobeyed the authority by refusing to accept the sultans overlordship or non-payment of the *Kharaj*, *Jaziya*[10] and other taxes, was severily dealt with.

Statistical Data of the Military Campaigns

S. No.	Sultan's Name	Campaigns Against		Percentage of Campaigns		Total Camp.	Objectives of Campaigns					Percentage of Obj.		Result	
		Hindus	Muslims	Hindus %	Muslims %		Pol.	Pol./ Eco.	Eco.	Rel.	Pol. Rel. %	Theo. %	Sec. %	Theo. %	Sec. %
(1)	(2)	(3)	(4)	(5)	(6)	(7)	(8)	(9)	(10)	(11)	(12)	(13)	(4)	(15)	(16)
1.	Qutabuddin Aibaq	5	3	62.50	37.50	8	8	—	—	—	—	—	100	31	69
2.	Shamsuddin Iltutmish	14	10	60	40	25	22	3	—	—	—	—	100	30	70
3.	Rukanuddin Ferozshah	—	8	—	100	8	8	—	—	—	—	—	100	—	100
4.	Raziya Begum	—	7	—	100	7	6	—	—	1	—	14.66	85.34	7	93

(Contd.)

(Contd.)

(1)	(2)	(3)	(4)	(5)	(6)	(7)	(8)	(9)	(10)	(11)	(12)	(13)	(14)	(15)	(16)
5.	Muizuddin Bahramshah	—	7	—	100	7	7	—	—	—	—	—	100	—	100
6.	Alauddin Masudshah	1	3	25	75	4	4	—	—	—	—	—	100	12	88
7.	Nasiruddin Mahmud	8	15	36.36	63.64	22	18	4	—	—	—	—	100	18	82
8.	Giyasuddin Balban	4	5	44.44	55.56	9	6	3	—	—	—	—	100	22	78
9.	Muizzuddin Quaiqubab	—	6	—	100	6	6	—	—	—	—	—	100	—	100
10.	Jalaluddin Khalji	6	5	54.54	45.46	11	6	2	—	2	1	27.27	72.73	41	59
11.	Alauddin Khalji	13	16	45	55	29	20	7	—	—	2	6.90	93.10	26	74
12.	Qutabuddin Khalji	2	7	28.57	71.43	9	7	2	—	—	—	—	100	14	86
13.	Nasiruddin Khurreshah	—	1	—	100	1	1	—	—	—	—	—	100	—	100
14.	Ghiyasuddin Tughluq	4	4	50	50	8	3	5	—	—	—	—	100	25	75

15. Muhammaddin Tughluq	14	37	27.45	72.55	51	31	16	13	1	—	2	98	15	85
16. Ferozshah Tughluq	15	10	60	40	25	8	6	—	—	10	40	60	50	50
17. Muhammadshah	4	10	28.56	71.44	14	13	1	—	—	—	—	100	14	68
18. Nasiruddin Mahmudshah	6	27	18.18	81.82	33	24	9	—	—	—	—	100	14	86
19. Khizr Khan	11	13	83	54.17	24	9	15	—	—	—	—	100	10	90
20. Muberkshah	2	3	40	60	5	5	—	—	—	—	—	100	20	80
21. Muhammadshah	—	3	—	100	3	3	—	—	—	—	—	100	—	100
22. Alauddinshah	—	1	—	100	1	1	—	—	—	—	—	100	—	100
23. Bahlollodhi	8	19	29.62	70.38	27	22	4	—	1	—	3.70	96.30	32	68
24. Sikandar Lodhi	14	17	45.16	54.84	31	20	5	—	1	5	19.35	80.65	32	68
25. Ibrahim Lodhi	4	11	26.67	73.33	15	14	—	—	—	—	6.67	93.33	17	83
Average of the 25 Sultan's Campaigns	136	246	35.55	64.45	382	272	82	3	7	18	6.54	93.46	21	79

Note : The figure .50 or above .50 is considered to be one in the respective side.

Index : Pol.=Political, Pol. and Eco.=Political and Economics, Rel.=Religions, Pol. Rel.=Political and Religions, Theoc.=Theocracy, Sec.=Secular.

The Sultans had hardly any regard for religion or religious beliefs during the course of their campaigns. In their private life some of them observed religious beliefs and practices such as praying in the Mosque, erection of new Mosques and repairing the old ones.

In case of the destruction of the Hindu places of worship, the motice was more greed for wealth than a *Jihad.* Again there are instances on the record then the temples were demolished only in the newly conquered territories or where those were constructed without the prior permission of Sultan.[11]

The Military operations of the Sultans resulted in loss of life and property in case of both the Hindus as well as Muslims. The conquerors motive was invariably greed for the precious metals than any religious real. The Hindus temples in medieval India (as even now) were noted for containing fabulous amount of the precious metals.[12] The first aim of the Sultans was always to fill their treasury. If the temples had been as simple as the Mosques, they would probably have not been the target of the sultans.

Summing up the whole arguments it may be inferred that the Sultans of Delhi carefully distinguished their public duties from their private faith. So far as public law is concerned, they imposed their sovereignty over all the subjects and they were not merely the rulers of their co-religionists. They did not feel morally concerned for the spiritual welfare of their non-Muslim subjects. The only demand of Sultans was due obedience from their subjects and regular payment of the state dues.

There are no instances to show if the conquered non-Muslims were disarmed or offered the choice of *Islam* or *Death*. On the contrary Sultans found all the Military campaigns a highly "hozardous task".[13] While non-Muslims did not tolerate any humiliation on the religious grounds, they were quite willing and ready to support the Sultan and accept his authority in political matters.

In the summing statistical data an attempt has been made to discuss the campaigns of the Sultans against Hindus as well as Muslims with their objectives and to evaluate the percentage

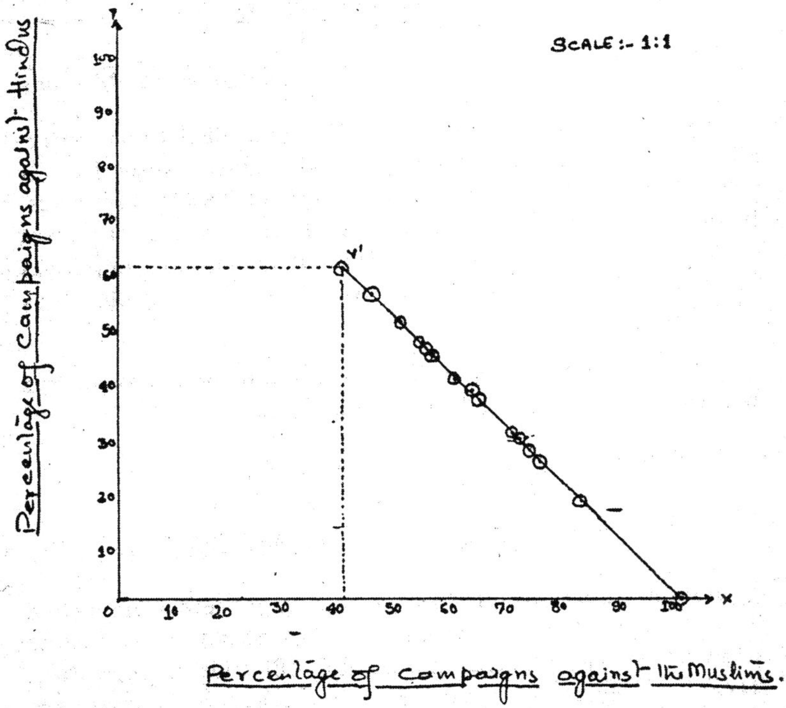

Fig. 1

of the both. On the basis of this data-evaluation we have tried to analyse the nature as to whether the state was a theocracy or secular during the early medieval period.

Analysis of the Data

Figure 1 shows a straight line (Y'X) is a decreasing which indicates that the percentage of campaigns against

Hindus inversely proportionate to the percentage of the campaigns against the Muslims.

As the rate of campaigns against Hindus increased, the rate of campaigns against Muslims decreased. Similarly when the rate of campaigns against Muslims increased the rate of campaigns against the Hindus decreased.

Therefore the percentage of campaigns against

$$\text{Hindus} \propto \frac{1}{\text{the percentage of campaigns against the Muslims}}$$

Figure 2 shows a straight line (Y′X) in a decreasing order, this indicates that percentage of theocratic objectives is inversely proportionate to the percentage of secular objectives. If the theocratic objectives increased the secular objectives shows a decline on the contrary when secular objectives increased the theocratic objectives shows a decline (as Y'X shows).

Therefore Y′O′ is decreasing line of the theocratic objectives whereas increasing line of secular objectives.

Therefore, the percentage of theocratic

$$\text{Objectives} \propto \frac{1}{\text{the percentage of secular objectives}}$$

Figure 3 shows a straight line and in a decreasing order. This indicates that the percentage of theocracy is decreasing whereas the percentage of secular objective is increasing. Therefore, again the percentage of theocracy is inversely pro portionate to the percentage of secularism which clearly shows the nature as only non-theocratic.

Therefore, percentage of theocratic

$$\text{Nature} \propto \frac{1}{\text{the percentage of secular nature}}$$

Figure 3 clearly indicate that the nature of the Sultanate is gradually increasing towards the secularism whereas the

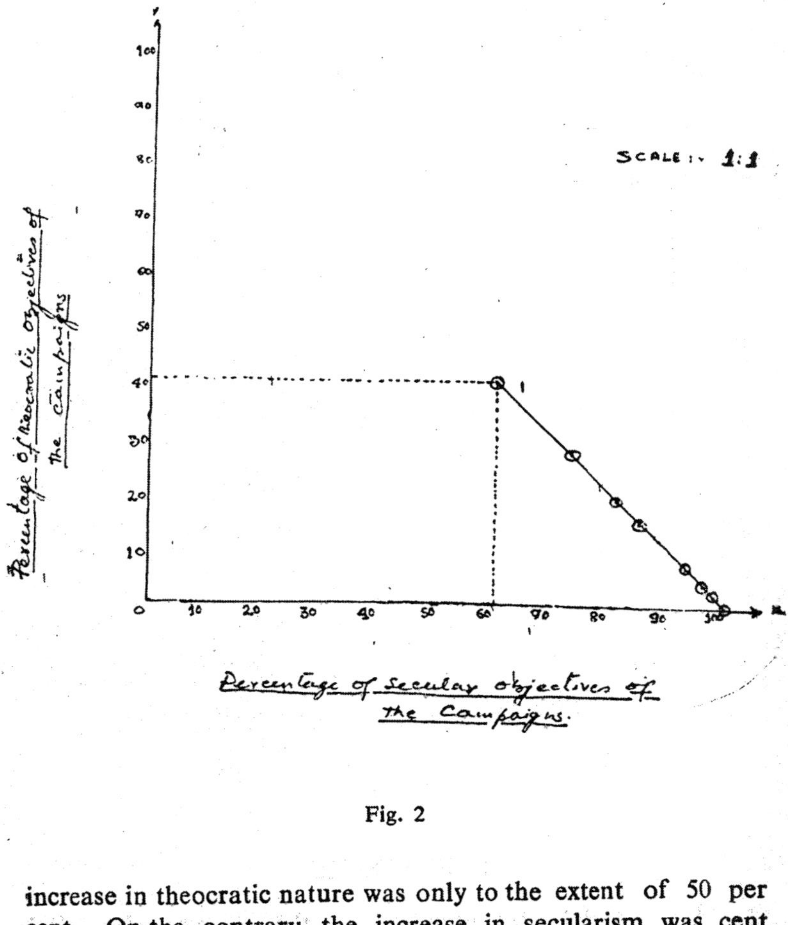

Fig. 2

increase in theocratic nature was only to the extent of 50 per cent. On the contrary the increase in secularism was cent per cent.

All data are therefore indicative of the fact that by and large the campaigns of the Sultans were secular in nature. Thus the nature of early medieval state in India was not theocratic but possible it will be secular. This is clearly revealed from the above statistical analysis and graphs of the campaigns led by the Sultans of Delhi.

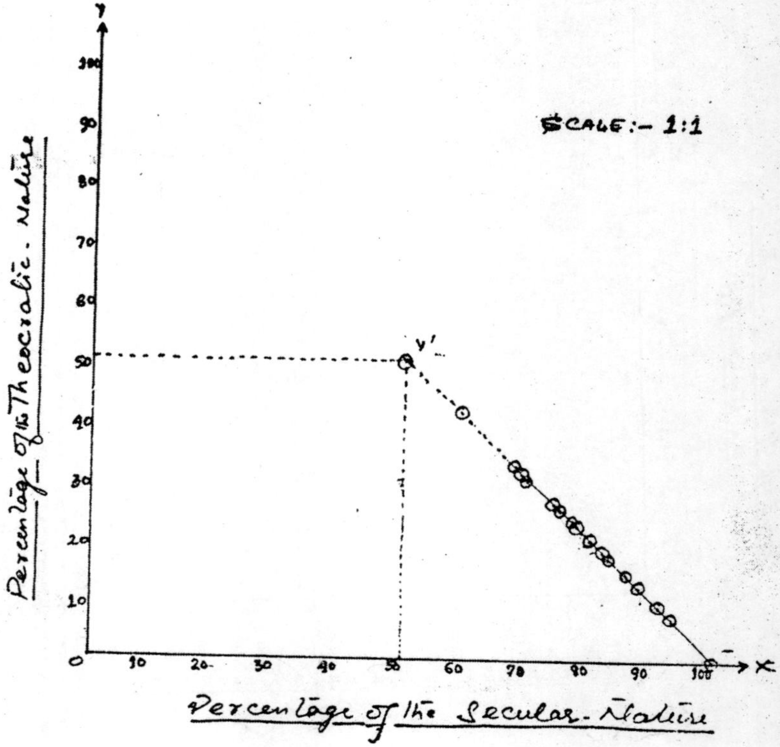

Fig 3

REFERENCES

1. Mohd. Habib, Introduction to the *Fatawa-i-Jahandari* pub. in, *Medieval India Quarterly*, Aligarh, 1958, Vol. III, p. 6.

2. R.P. Tripathi, *Some Aspects of Muslim Administration*, Allahabad, 1964, p. 2. He is followed by others modern writers such as T.P. Huges, *Dictionary of Islam*, New Delhi, 1971, p. 711 ; *Encyclopaedia of Islam*, Vol. I, p. 959 ; K.S. Lal, *Studies in Medieval Indian History*, Delhi, 1966, p. 156.

3. The essential feature of theocracy—the rule of an ordained priesthood is however, missing in organisation of Muslim State. The Jurists are all laymen who claimed no sacere-dotal immunity from error. I.H. Qureshi, *The Administration of the Sultanate of Delhi*, New Delhi, 1971, p. 44.

4. *Sea-Medieval India Quarterly*, Aligarh, 1958, Vol. III, p. 6.

5. *Ibid.*, p. 6, see also K.A. Nizami (ed.), *Politics and Society During Early Medieval Period.* 1974, Vol. I, pp. 16-17.

6. See the statistical table as prepared in page 3, 4 and 5 shown on the graph paper figures 1, 2, 3.

7. For example see Barani, *Tarikh-i-Ferozshahi* Calcutta text, pp. 211-12 ; 509-11 ; Islami, *Futuh-us-Salatin*, Madras, 1948, pp. 117-21 ; Amir Khurd, *Siyar-ul-Kuliya*, Delhi, 1885, pp. 527-29, etc.

8. For example—the leading Ulama of the realm suggested Sultan Iltutmish that he will not only collect *Jaziya* and *Kharaj* from the Hindus but also followed the policy of *Death or Islam.* He tackles the situation very tactfully—Barani, *Sahifainat-i-Muhammadi*, Rampur Raza Lib., pp. 391-92. cited in, *Adi Turk Kalin Bharat*, Aligarh, 1958, pp. 107-108.

9. See for example—Alauddin's discourse with Qazi Mugis-uddin' of Bayana, Barani, *op. cit.*, pp. 289-96 ; Sultan Mohammad-bin-Tuglaq's discourse with Ulama, Yahaya, *Tarikh-i-Mubarkshahi*, Calcutta, 1931, pp. 115-116.

10. See for example—Prince Mohammad of Balban's campaigns of Damrila and Nagarkot-Amir Khusaru, *Diwan-i-Wastul-Hayat*, Aligarh, n.d., p. 145.

11. Ferozshah Tughlaq demolished the temples in Malwah, Salehpur, Gohana and Tughliqpur, *Futuhat-i-Ferozshahi*, Aligarh, 1954, pp. 9-10.

12. Jalaluddin Khalji demolished and plundered the temples of Jain. See for detail—A. Khusrau, *Miftah-ul-Futuh*, Aligarh, 1954, pp. 31-32 ; Alauddin's campaigns of Bhilsa-Barani, *op. cit.*, p. 220 ; Alauddin Khalji's collection of riches from the Som Nath and other temples of South India—Barani, pp. 251, 325-41 ; A. Khusrau, *Khazain-ul-Futuh*, Aligarh, 1927, pp. 50-53, 70-180.

13. A.B.M. Habibullah, *Foundation of Muslim Rule in India*, Allahabad, 1976, p. 266.

2

Working Class During the Delhi Sultanate

The working class in born with the existent of the social difference in the society. In the beginning "labour" word was not used to its full extent. The small farmers, slavish hand workers or small artisitians from the backbone of nation's economy. It is because the industries are based on the labour of peasants and workers. In this manner workers is the backbone of the national economy. During the ancient times self-sufficiency and economic condition were based on the works of the workers, so was it in the medieval period. Because these workers used to fullfil the demands of their owner or so called state or the ruler.

Before describing the positions of workers during Delhi Sultanate, it is necessary to know about the establishment of the Sultanate in brief. It was established in 1206 A.D. by the first Sultan Qutabuddin Aibak and came to an and with the establishment of the Mughal Empire by the first emperor Babur in 1526 A.D. From 1206 A.D. to 1526 A.D., about to 320 years the Sultanate was ruled over by the different Sultans of different dynasties such as—Early-Turks, Khalji, Tughluq, Sayyiad and Lodi Sultans. The whole region of Sultan known as Sultanate period.

First of all, it would be facite to the subject to know that who formed this class. Generally, "Workers" imply the "hard working people". But during the Sultanate period it had varied implications such as slaves, industrial (here means only *Karkhana*) workers, professional-workers, peasants. It will be obvious to describe the works and position of all these different workers. We are fully aware of the economic importance of the workers. Thus keeping their importance and present workers-problems in view, they have choosen for the study so that we may know the origin of this problem. But our present papers are limited only to the extent of Delhi Sultanate.

It is necessary to know about the 'Slave' work first then the slave class. Actually the word "slave" is a variation of the "Slav"[1] word. Gradually this word was used in the 18th century because number of Slave-people were taken slaves in the Europe.[2] In this way the slavery is the result of Medieval feudalism in Europe but the condition of slaves in India seems a different. It (Slavery) ows a approval in India in the ancient law-books written in Sanskrit. In *Manusanhita*[3] in the description of the seven causes of slavery is given—they are war-captives, basters, bought slaves *Krit Das*, presented or inherrited slaves, willingly surrendering slave in lieu of protecotion and reproached slaves. In this way *Manusanhita* gives approval of slavery during the ancient times. In the same manner the *Sudras* plight and Brahmins reproach can be traced upto *purushsukat*, which is marital song of *Rigavenda*, is written about the slave that they have sprung from the foot of a man.[4] 'Foot' means the service, hence, the slavery in India started from the very ancient times.

The approval of slave and slavery institution was also provided to Muslim society from the earliest times[5] of which detailed description is given in the *Quran*[6]. Prophet Mohammad has accepted the slavery without any hesitation or interference but in the *Hadis* sympathy towards the slaves has been shown to some extent. From the above description we can conclude that the slavery was existing in India during the Ancient and Medieval periods.

Manusanhita gives the seven methods of slave making. In the same manner there were three ways to make slaves during the medieval period—Bought or Barter-slaves, secondly, war-captives people could be converted into the slaves. Thirdly, a family or a tribe who failed to repay the loan or tax payer could be converted into slaves as long as he did not pay back money. He has to work for his money-lender or his owner. But in the passage of time these money-lenders took unpaid labour or *Begar* and did not let them free. This process gave a birth to the hereditory-slaves. Both the men and women could be kept as slaves.

Second, category of workers is that of industrial or professional-workers. During the Delhi Sultanate its implication was too narrow. There were no large-scale or like modern scientific industries, but industrial workers means only those who used to work in the *Karkhanas*[7] of Sultans or Amirs. Besides this the professional workers also used to live in the villages such as Blacksmiths, Goldsmiths, carpenters, cobbers, potters, weavers, Barbers, etc. All these workers used to earn their living on the basis of their professions. It would not be wrong to call them "Professional Workers" because they used to use their profession as a means to livelihood. These workers were adopting their profession on paternal basis. Therefore, there was a perfection in their articles or profession. On the basis of this perfection in their articles, they can be classified into two classes—skilled and unskilled workers, vicissitudinarily-Blacksmiths, Goldsmiths, Barbers, Weavers formed the skilled class and collies farm-labourers, unpaid labourers or *Begar*, Sweepers, paddy-workers were kept in the unskilled class.

Peasant were the third class of workers during the Delhi Sultanate. The nature of agrarian system during Sultanate was too complex. Most of the dinizens of the Sultanate used to dwell in the rural area and agriculture was their main profession. Luxurious and rich people kept a far from this profession. Thus rulers also did not take much interest to improve their living standard. Consequently, the peasants remained a pray to poverty, disgrace and inequality.[8] Turks or Delhi Sultans,

Amirs and Chief's had great interest in urbanisation. It also shows that they did not pay sufficient heed towards the development of agriculture. But to seek the co-operation of their 'amirs, sultan' distributed the lands to their *amir* or *maliks* in the form of *Iqtas* and *Muqtas.* These amirs or *Iqtadar* or *Muqtai* did not cultivate the land themselves but land used to be cultivated by peasants. In other words, peasants were the sole cultivators of land.

Distribution of lands by the conquerors or Delhi Sultanate arise a question that how many type of land holding was there? During the Sultanate period there were three types of land holding. Firstly, *Iqta Land*—This was a type of land which was distributed by Turks conquerors to their *amirs* in lieu of the cash payment and keeping military for their rulers services. Secondly, *tributary-lands*—where the defeated king or chief used to pay the 'tribute' to the conqueror. It was fixed by the conqueror, on this account victorious privileged him to rule over the region. Thiidly, was the *Khalisu Lands*—which were directly under the control of *Wazarat* department or central government. It's revenue was collected by the Sultan's officials and used to deposit in the royal treasury.[9]

From the above three types of land arised problem of ownership of land that who was the owner of land ? In India from the time in memorial the land had belonged to the people and not to the king. Late Dr. Jaiswal, however, as early as 1924, had threshed out the question quite at length. His findings led him to conclude that the property in the soil rested with cultivator not with king. "It is emphatically declared that the king has no property in the soil and that is declared in no less an authority than the very logic of Hindu Law the *Mimamsa.*[10] The Hindu Law provided that a conquest ownership of the conqueror extended only to the house land and property of the conquered. The conqueror got the right of taxation but no ownership of the soil of the people. After this Dr. P. Saran also confirmed that, "The king enjoyed only *usufructuary* rights in the land and not proprietory rights. He could, therefore, transfer only those rights which he possessed and nothing more".[11] No doubt, the Turkis conquest had destroyed the Hindu-Monarchy but by the circumstances they were not capable of uprooting the cultivators.

In the three types of land—cultivators had been cultivated the land not the *Iqtadars, Sultans, Amirs*. Prof. Irfan Habid has rightly remarked that, "Peasants is related to land and land is related to the peasants". As Turks were military conquerors, foreigners in the beginning and very few in number almost all of them soldiers. To settle the soldiers on the land as peasants would have jeopardised their own position. Perhaps some of the land would had been cultivated by the landless-workers because land owner had a vast fields or area of their holding. The need of an extra labour would arise to sowing the seeds and to collect crops and separate the grains. Only unskilled-workers could provide the extra-labour. Peasants were divided into three categories on the basis of their ownership of land and land holdings.[12]

Therefore, we can say that the three categories of workers such as slave, prefessional or industrial workers and peasants were the real owner of production. It means that in the period of our study the production was based on the workers-labour. In this way, workers were the main basis of economic set-up during the Sultanate but what was the situation of workers ? The origin of the working class during Delhi Sultanate, was due to the setting of bureaucratic administration and welfare of subject according to the circumstances. Slavery remained due to the elements of bureaucracy, compulsory and unpaid-labour or *Begar* from the poors. Secondly, it remained because of the many way of slave-making such as war-captives, bought from the markets, due to poverty or unable to repay the debt, etc.

If the slave was war-captive his life and position would be at the mercy of the captor, conqueror or the Sultan. If he was a bought-slave, the transferee or *Kreta*, had proprietory rights over him. He could gave him as a present to any body. The worker was paid for his labour but a slave on other hand, had no such rights. He had to do all sorts of work good or bad of his owner.[13] His civil rights were based on the generosity or Will of his owner. They used to live under the lordship of their owners.

It has been described earlier that both men and women could be made slaves. The approval is given to both types of slaves in the *Quran.* Slavey or *Dassi* were categorically divided into three classes on the basis of their work-performance and beauty. First, *Qari-Qanniz*—who used to do ordinary works, second, *Qinnari-Qanniz* who were cute and beautiful; third, *Qari-Qinnari-Qanniz* who were expert in ordinary works, cute and beautiful females. In the same way slaves or *Dass* also formed three categories according to their performance and smartness[14].

Slavey or *Dassi* were assigned ordinary work used to be unskilled and they had to face humiliation in every way. On the other hand, the cute and beautiful women who used to be bought for luxury were respectful. Sometimes they even influenced the Royal family or *Haram* such as after the death of Sultan Shamsuddin Iltutmish, Shah-Turkan had paricularly influence in his *haram,* who was a converted slavey or *Dassi.* Similary, Maulana Shams a'sadi was so much influenced by a slavey or *dassi* that he was mad after her.[15]

In the Sultanate period, the prices of these bought slaves and salveys were to settle according to their smartness, cute, beauty and working capacity. According to Ziauddin Barani's description, *Qari Qanniz* was 5 to 12 *tankas*; *Qinnari-Qanniz.* was 20 to 30 *tankas* and *Qari-Qinnari-Qanniz* was 40 to 50 *tankas.* In the same way the slave-*Qarkarda* prices was 10 to 15 *tankas,* servant slaves 7 to 8 *tankas* and the off springs of a handsome slave was 20 to 30 *tankas.* The prices of a handsome slave varied between 100 to 200 *tankas.*[16] For example, Iltutmish was so handsome that Mohammad Ghori had banned his sale in Ghazani. After all Qutbuddin Aibak bought him from an ancestress of Sultan Ghori in the Delhi slave-market for 1500 *tankas.*[17]

Our poet-historian Hazarat Amir Khusrau's description also shows that, *Jariye* and *Khidmati* were used to be sweepers and grinders.[18] And in the home they had generally to help their owner in washing their hands, cook and serve the meals.[19] They were also means of livelihood or earnings for their owners as Amir Hasan Sijji writes that Maulana Noor Turk[20] had a slave who used to weave cotton clothes and to pay one *dirham* every day to his owner which was a sort of means of livlihood to Maulana Noor-Turk.[21] Another slave used to give to his owner one third of his income from his manual labour.[22]

Some Sultans had appointed slaves as a *Chashnigar*[23], *Saqi-i-Khas*[24] and *Sar-i-A'bdar*[25], etc. When Sultan Alauddin Khalji introduced the market regulations he used to appointed these slaves to check the prices of different goods.[26] We know from the Ibn i-Batutta's *Rehla* that Sultan Muhammad-bin-Tughluq had appointed his slaves at every *Amir's* and *Malik's* court to know about their activities, who used to acquaint the Sultan with each and every activity of *Amir* or *Malik*. Slavey or *Dassi* were also used to spy for him.[27]

Sultan took full advantage of slaves faithfulness by appointing them as his body-guards as Ferozshah Tughluq had 10,000 slaves in his protection army who used to watch his palace.[28] Similarly, there always used to be 40,000 slaves with Sultan Muhammad-bin-Tughluq.[29] The traders or business man also did the same by keeping slaves as their boatsmen and body guards.[30]

The slaves also used to play an active role in the contemporary politics such as Muhammad Ghori appointed Qutabuddin Aibak, Nasiruddin Quabacha and Tajuddin Yaldoz as his subordinates respectively in the newly conquered territories of India at Lahore, Kamran and Sankuran on the route from Afghanistan to upper Sind and Ucch. Aibak even made expansions in his Patron's or Sultan's empire in the latter's absence.[31] After the death of Sultan Shamsuddin Iltutmish, his successors failed to establish the law and order as well as stability in the administration due to the hectic political activities and interferences of *Turkan-i-chehlgani* or "the group of forty slaves".[32]

Owing to his unique administrative talent and statemanship Balban became the Sultan of the Sultanate from an ordinary slave.[33] Similarly, Malik Kafur was a reliable Malik of Sultan Alauddin Khalji, on whose instigations Sultan arrested his own son Khizr Khan. The slaves were also appointed on important positions in the Tughluq Sultanate such as Imad'ul-Mulk was on a high rank in the Sultan Ferozshah's military.[34] In this way the slaves of Sultans played an active role in the contemporary politics due to the sympathetic attitude of the Sultans. Their co-operative attitude became a decisive element in the acquisition of throne.[35]

The cissy-slaves used to work in the *harams* of the Sultans. The literary works used to be assigned to the unbearded and slavey or *Dassi* Barani writes that "beautiful slavey or *Dassi* were used to be trained in the field to sing a song and keep the decorum of court or so that they could please the luxurious Sultans like the Muizzuddin Quiqubad".[36] A few slaveys or *Dassian* remembered the Quran orally. Everyday, they used to play for five times and observe fasts or *Rozah*[37] Becomming versed in different fine arts many slave became professional artists[38].

Like the slaves professional workers were also assigned the important duties. The trade and commerce, construction or production and the development of the state was based upon their work. They were divided into skilled and unskilled groups. The weavers, masons, blacksmiths, sculptor, barbers, goldsmiths, engravars, etc., formed the skilled professional worker group. The unskilled on was formed by the coolies, unpaid workers or *Begaries* washermen, paddy-men, archers, *Khidmatis*, etc. These workers worked on geneological basis. Their tools used to be rough and peculiar tyre. Due to this geneological basis they achieved the perfection in their profession. The production was not too much, because their production was only limited to the demands of aristocrates or amirs as Bengal and Devgiri were requsted for their silk production.

Some of them used to work in the royal or Sultan's *Karkhons*. The description about these workers involvement found but unfortunately the rate of their wages are not mentioned by the any chroniclers. Generally the state used to keep the production and distribution of all goods and things free from its control.[39] It was only Sultan Alauddin Khalji in the Sultanate period who dared to set up the bold step to control the Delhi market. His aim was more politically motivated then what it seemed economically inspired.[40]

Indian weavers skill has an enough proof of their perfection among which Deogiri, Devgiri, Mahadevgiri, Bengal fabrics were having world fame. Metal artist, sculptor, Mason, were known for their art. Our poet-historian Amir Khusrau has written about them that, "The Mason and Sculptors of Delhi were the most reputed one's in the whole Muslim World".[41] It can be guessed from the existing monuments of art and memorable buildings of Sultanate, that how skilled they would have been in the field or art.

Some .workers used to work on small scale such as leather-work, sugar-work, ivory-work, etc. The used to produce according to the demands of the people but they had to be pray to the atrocities of the Amirs, traders or business men. They wore not paid even approximate price for their labour. On other hand, the unskilled workers were less paid in the comparision of their labour, with which they could hardly make their both ends meet. Generally, professional workers to fulfil the demands of the nobility and Sultan not for the common subject of the Sultanate.

On other hand, Turks Sultans and his co-ordinators were, no doubt, urban settler, had a particular interest in town-establishment. The examples of which are the existing dozens of town in Delhi. The production was nominal but romance and luxury pervaded in the towns. These town would had to be depend upon the near by villages for the fulfilment of their demands. Prof. Irfan Habib has righly said at such condition that villages were self-sufficient and they did not bring any thing from the town. Hence these workers[42] did not think of producing for the society at large because, had they done so ? They would have to exploited at the hands of nobility, traders and businessman. They would not get an adequate prices for their products so as state had no protection for them.

The peasants had the most important place in economy. It was only their hard work which resulted into the self sufficiency in the villages. Secondly, "Kharaj" or land revenue was the main source of the state income according to the Muslim Law of taxation. If the crops be good, it is obvious that the state will get more *Kharaj*. The rate of *Kharaj* varied according to the different Sultans of Delhi Sultanate.[43] Even though it can be concluded that it was 1/3 to 1/2 of the total produce.[44]

The peasants used to hard word in their fields, especially during the sowing and harvesting seasons. They had to work by day and night. Much of their produce was given as *Kharaj* and inform of other taxes, and from the rest of the produces a specific quantity had to be given to the other workers[45] and servants who used to provide them the tools and articles of their necessity. In this way, with the balance grains they use to feed their family. Thus a great part of their hard-earned grains was collected in the form of different taxes and he could seldom make his both ends meet for the whole year. The peasant was considered blessed who ate his belly full for the whole year.

Shamsu Siraj Afif has written about the agricultural produce and condition of peasants, that "every year peasants profit started increasing in comparison to the present. All peasants became affluent and were free from worries. The work load of the peasants reached to such extent if he would sow a hand full of grain, he would get from seventy to seven hundred or more in return.[46] By this description if seems that the peasants who had left the agriculture during the reign of Muhammad-bin-Tughluq must had started taking interest in agriculture. As a result of which the production must have increased and peasants must have been having sufficient grain for their livelihood.

Secondly, the peasants suffered loss after every invasion, the soldiers of victorious army used to plunder the conquered regions. Contemporary and non-contemporary chronicles are full of such examples. The soldiers did not care for the crops during the campaigns. Consequently, the economic condition of the peasants was disrupted. They had also to face natural calamities such as when Sultan Muhammad-bin-Tughluq increased the rate of taxes in Doab region, in he same year a calamity fell on them and the year happened to be dry one. At that time the officials proved harsh in collecting the taxes. Therefore, peasants ran away, giving up their lands.[47]

In this way the works of the different categories of the workers show that in every sphere the interest and disinterests of the Sultanate was involved. Moreover, the Sultans overlooked their interests and never paid sufficient attentions to improve their (workers) living standards. If some one protected their interests so to what extent ? First of all, the slave workers used to do the political, social, security, military, cultural and literary works of the Sultan. Therefore, they were helpful to the political stability, establishment of peace and orders, and development of the sultanate. If a slave had been a captive, his life was at the mercy of his captor. If he had been a bought slave or *Krit* the transferee *Kreta* had proprietory rights upon him. So none of the clever transferee or "Kreta" would neglect such property. He would not error in his bringing-up, so that he could be converted into more-profitable one's. According to a decree, "If the Sultan wanted to free any slave, he also had to give compensation to his owner".[48] Sultan Ferozshan Tughluq ordered his provincial officials if they presented him a slave. They should take his price from the "Kharaj".[49] It shows that state had recognised the property consisting of slaves as personal property.

In other public places the slave was not considered as a free man in the eyes of Muslim Law or *Shara.* He could not appoint as a *Qazi*, *Imam* of any place or *Sultan* of state unless he could not get the *Emancipation-letter*. He can be punished only in the presence of his owner.[50] According to Rizqullah

Mushtaqi, "If a slave failed to get his accounts cleared from his owner, he could request the Sultan for the justice. His accounts cleared and justice imparted to him none could get unpaid labour or "begar" from any one".[51] Sultan Gyasuddin Balban whipped Malik Baqbak for killing a slave by which the Malik died.[52] Similarly, Haibat Khan had to bear vigorous punishment because of the death of a slave.[53]

The Sultans of Delhi Sultanate had given full protection to the slaves. They always had a large group of slaves which presented with them. They impressed the sultan with their respective abilities and gradually promoted to the rank of *Amir*, *Malik*, *Khan* and even *Sultan* such as Qutabuddin Aibak, Shamsuddin Iltutmish and Gyasuddin Balban who became *Sultan* from a slave or (appointed) *Bhishti*.[54] In the same way, slaves such as Khusrau Khan, Imadul-Mulk, Malik Kafur acquired an important position with their abilities in the nobility or *Umra-class*. Thus, the Sultan's slaves enjoyed a better deal then ordinary one's. They had an adequate protection from the state as well as exercised the powers.

Possibly in the same way the plight of the slaves of amirs or businessmen and traders would have been in accordance with their economic position, as the slaves assigned the duty of body guards and boat-men. The slave of Sheikh Noor Turk was the means of his livelihood. Sultan Muhammad-bin-Tughluq used to distribute 2 *mans* wheet and rice every month, two *seers* meat everyday and the articles of daily needs to the every slave. Besides this he distribute one hundred *tankas* and four pair of clothes every year.[55]

Sultan Muhammad-bin-Tughluq used to arrange the marriages of the slave-girls and boys aftermancipating them. The Sultan Ferozshah Tughluq established a seperate department *Sahib i-Bandgan* to protect the interests of the slaves. Different official of this department were appointed. He distributed areas of different *Vilayats* among them and provided sufficient arrangements for their technical or industrial training. He issued a decree to the *amirs* and *maliks* that they must make the arrangements to trained the slaves in different fields of fine arts and must submit the yearly progress report to Sultan. Inspite of this, he provides them allowances for six, four and three months respectively 100, 50, 30, 25 and 10 *tankas*.[56]

No description is available about the *Early Turks Sultans* of Delhi Sultanate. On the basis of which we can conclude regarding the slaves. Possibly, the policy which was adopted by the Tughluq Sultans must have been continued from the reign of the *Early Turk Sultan* because they were themselves slaves before the appointment as a Sultan. By which some historians name it the "Reign of Slave-Dynasty". Later on they were given the *Emancipation-letter* by their owner or Sultan. Secondly, after the death of Sultan Iltutmish, *Turkan-i-Chehlgani* or a group of forty slaves were active in the politics by which the successors of former Sultan could not rule with stability. Possibly the slave would have been having protection from the begining. Therefore, they had the opportunity to show their dexterity and ability. Through the persistant progress they became the Sultan of Sultanate. Thus the protection of the slaves interest during the Delhi Sultanate would have been according to the social and economic position of their protector.

No doubt, professional-workers were responsible for the production. They either produced by borrowing money from the money-lenders or used to bear the production expenses on their own part. During Medieval period, it can be judged from the active role of money-lenders, traders and businessmen in the production capacity, that they had control over the production capacity. Responsibility of production of the workers led to the self-sufficiency in the village community. They always keep in view the demands of nobility, Sultan as well as other rich one's. The protection was not given to the interests of the experts and workers except those who were appointed in the royal *Karkhanas*.[57]

Due to the limited economic means and social conditions, the village artisans could progress to a certain limit. Because if they directly produce for markets would have been exploited by the business-men or traders. Where they had their sole-right. Secondly, being burned with the loans of landlords and Money-lenders they did not sell their articles or goods on appropriate prices. They used to purchase more articles on low prices. Because of which the village-articians could not make development. Pointing towards the exploitation of the businessmen and traders Barani writes that, "Businessmen or traders were the sole proprietors of all the articles. They used to buy and sell at their own will".[58]

Consequently, it can be concluded about the professional-workers or *Karkhana's* workers that possibly only those one working in the Sultan's *Karkhanas* were provided protection but there, too was the interest of ruler involved and not of the workers. It can be guessed at the rest of workers position that they had to bear the atrocities of the business community and money-lenders. In that period the policy such as the increase in production, protection to the worker's benefits were beyond the jurisdiction of the Sultanate's administrative policy.

During the Sultanate period most of the people were engaged in agricultural activities. Secondly, *Kharaj* was the main source of state income. The small cottage industry and artisan's profession were based upon the peasants labour.[59] In other words, land was related to the peasants and peasants were related to the land. Considering the importance of peasantry Gyasuddin Balban gave attention to protect their interests. Sultan Alauddin Khalji punished the corrupt officials of the *Diwon-i-Wazarat* to protect the peasants from their exploitations. Keeping in view the importance of peasants, Ghiysuddin Tughluq once remarks that peasants formed the back-bone of the state. What policy did adopt for the peasants? How for did the Sultans of Sultanate protect their interests?

Contemporary or non-contemporary chroniclers of Delhi Sultanate are silent about the village organisation. There can be two reasons for the silence—Firstly, these chroniclers were not interested in the village organisation. Their chronicles were confined to the activities of the court and nobility. Secondly, these chroniclers failed to understand the land-organisation and also left the subject of village organisation untouched. So in the abosence of factual knowledge in the sources, we can only infere that the state of agriculture remained more or less unchanged till the 13th century because the Sultans spent most of their time in military campaigns, in suppressing the rebels. As a result, they could not interfere the agricultural system. Therefore, the peasants did not feel the need of knowing that who was charging the how much revenue ?

Balban was the first sultan who adopted a moderate policy towards the peasants. Barani writes, "The peasants should not be over charged with the excess of revenue. The administration should be strong and just. A moderate policy should be adopted in fixing the revenue because overcharging leeds to poverty of the state, but too low rate of the revenue also makes them lazy and unrestrained. Therefore, its urgent that the peasants should possess enough to feed himself but he should not have so much as to make him a rebel".[60] We come to know that Balban ordered a medium policy to be adopted towards the peasants. But our chronicler Barani's statement has some inconsistencies regarding the *Kharaj* Policy that was prevailed before this. It does not say anything about the condition of peasants. Even so, the statement has importance as it tells us about the Balban's policy towards the peasants.

Sultan Alauddin Khalji adopted a new land revenue policy to appease his high ambitions that half portion of the crops were accessed as "Kharaj". All the *Kharaj-privilages* of *Maliks* and *Amirs* were dispossed. The method of measurement was adopted to access the *Kharaj.* Two taxes named as *Charai* and *Karai* were also imposed.[61] The collection of fifty percent of the total produce as a *Kharaj* was really a severe rule. After the implementation of the market regulations peasants were ordered to sell their surplus produce to the traders at the rates fixed by the government. As a result of this, the peasants will ceased to take active interest in agriculture because they could not get remunerative price for their hard earned crops.

There was an increase in the poverty of the peasants due to the strict policy of the Sultan. But Alauddin Khalji ordered his revenue officials (such as Patwari) to keep a record of revenues. The peasants of *Khalisa Lands* were in direct contact with *Diwan-i-Wazarat's* officials. The peasants in the provinces were contected through "Subedars" and his officials. Any how, the interests of the peasants were patronaged by giving them freedom to lodge complaints against the corrupt officials and severelly punishing the quilty one's. As a result, the nobles of his nobility were also treated at par with the other peasants. But the incapable successor of Alauddin Khalji did not continue this strict policy by which this policy ended with the Alauddin's reign.

Sultan Ghiyasuddin Tughluq ordered about the assessment of *Kharaj* with *Batai* system in keeping view the conditions of crops and introducing certain changes in prevailing system of taxation.[62] His ideal of reform was based on the development of agriculture and peasants. Sultan Muhammad-bin-Tughluq stricitly ordered the collection of taxes by increasing the rate of the tax in Doab region, but the peasants left the cultivation of land because of the rigid behaviour of the revenue officials and the Natural calamities. As a result, sultan was forced to change his policy a seperate department *Diwan-i-Kohi*[63] was established to develop the agriculture and loans were given to peasants towards the state. The experiment of rotation-croping was done[64] which was an impossible project for the Europeans at that time. *Shiqdars* were appointed for the protection of peasants but even then sultan failed to improve their condition.

Sultan Ferozshah Tughluq tried to abolish the repressing policy by accepting the welfare of the peasants the welfare of the state. He also tried to improve their economic condition. He ordered that *Kharaj* should be assessed on the basis of the actual produce. The revenue officials were directed not to collect any thing except *Kharaj*. They were give an rebate of two *Jitals*, per *tankas*. The officials of provinces were asked, "To deduct the price of presents from the *Kharaj*, if ever they sent him presents because the peasants had to bear this burden indirectly.[66] Canals were laid down to increase the cultivation of land. It must be contributed to the development of agriculture, as it is clear from the chronicle of Afif.[67]

During the Afgan's Sultanate the interests of peasants were guaranteed by the ruler. According to Mushtaqi, "Agriculture was main source of state income. The Sultan encouraged every body for cultivation of land. By which the forests were cut down and cultivation was done on rural and urban land. Villages were rehabilated and the land turned into the grainaries.[68] Peasants were also encouraged to cultivate the *Banjar* lands. They were given loans by the state inform of economic aid. In this way agriculture was in developed form during the reign of Sikander Lodhi. Abdullah the writer of *Tarikh-i-Daudi* had also confirmed this account[69].

From an account of *Tarikh-i-Shershahi*, which is written by Abbas Khan Sharwani, we came to know that Farid (later known as Shershah Suri) understood very well the importance of cultivators. He established the contacts with peasants and gave them a choice to assess the revenue according to measurement or *Batai* system. He issued them the letters of *Patta* for the ownership of land and *Qabuliyat* to pay the assessed revenue. The rebelious peasants were severely dealt with. He ordered the revenue officials to adopt a policy—be libeıal to the peasants at the time of assessment but be rigid at the time of collection.[70]

Thus, from the above study we come to the conclusion that the different sultans took interest in agriculture in different ways according to their inclination and ambitions and to protect the interests of peasants accordingly. Their vested interests were also involved. Therefore, they failed to fully protect the agriculture and the interests of peasants. Political instability, rebellions, ruthlessness of the soldiers during military campaign adversly effected the peasants, destroyed their crops and ransacked their grains.[72] So the peasants were made victims of the bims of soldiers, officials and the sultans. They had also to suffer the tyrannies of administration. The poet-historian Amir

Khusrau seems to have rightly observed that, "Each pearl of the crown of ruler, is a drop of perspiring, weeping eyes of the peasants and is a drop of their blood.[73]

Even so, it looks from a critical analysis of the sources of the Sultanate period that "*Karkhanas*" provided work to the workers at a small scale by taking away some part of the labour to the administration. Possibly, workers might not have been able to get a two square meals a day after putting a day's hard and continuous labour. The protection of the intersts of workers working in *Shahi Karkhanas* and on *Khal.sa Lands* was provided by the state and the rest of the workers seems to be outside the state policy. They were left on the mercy of liberal or cruel attitude of their landlords or owners.

Generally, the worker is a basic and essential part of any production procedure. It is by labour that man sows the seeds of nature and has a control and regulation over them. The labour of workers create physical wealth. To secure the protection of their intersts which were not safe in the Sultanate and because of the perpetual struggle between rulers and exploited-class. The workers took active part in the contemporary politics. The resistance and non-co-operation was a natural reaction because the protector (Ruler) did not have any sympathy for them. By these conditions Sultans of different dynasties ruled over the Delhi Sultanate. Consequently, the Sultanate disintegrated into small states. The rulers of these states sought the co-operation of the workers on their cost basis. This internal fighting led to the establishment of Mughal-Empire.

Repression and exploitation of the workers was probably one of the causes of downfall of Delhi Sultanate. First, the workers stood by Sultans, Amir and Maliks in the hope of protecting their interest but when they felt that they could not get protection, they turned hostile to them as happened after the death of Iltutmish—an atmosphere of uncertainity and political instability prevailed till 1246 A.D. due to the active interference of *Turkan-i-Chehlgani.* Similarly the workers joined hand with Jalaluddin Khalji when they became fed up with the tyranny of Malik Nizamuddin and the indifferent attitude of the Sultan Muizzuddin Qaiqubad, who led them for his selfish motives. The Sultanate period is full of such examples of the rebellious maliks and workers also contributed indirectly to them (because they had a direct contact with these workers). At the time of the decline of Sultanate the workers were mainly divided into two groups, one led by Sultan Ibrahim Lodhi and other by Daulat Khan Lodhi. Besides this they organise themselves under the leadership of many other petty amirs, maliks and cheiftains. The Hindu workers organised themselves under the leadership of Rana Sanga of Mewar.

The clever maliks, amirs and cheiftains made the use of the discontentment of the workers against the exploited class and became their leaders. They owned the responsibility of rebellions. It is right to remark here that they were also motivated by their vested interests. At least not last, we can say that the lack of protection of workers interests led to the downfall of the Delhi Sultanate. By which they used to change their sympathy and co-operation and were the determining factor in the stability of the Delhi Sultanate while Sultanate generally ignored them.

REFERENCES

1. The resident of Eastern Europe means-Russia, Bulgaria, Illeria, Poland, Pomerenia, Bohemia, regions, etc., known as the "Slav".
2. *Encyclopaedia of the Social Sciences*, New York, 1959, Vol. XIII-XIV, p. 77.
3. *Mannus Sanhita*, Pt. VIII, p. 415.
4. *Rigaved*, Pt. X, p. 90.
5. The main features of slavery in Muslim World see *Encyclopaedia of the Social Sciences*, *op. cit.*, p. 79.

6. For detail see *Quran*, Ch. IV, 3, 28, 29, 40 ; Ch., 49, Ch. XXIII, 5, Ch. XXIV, 33, Ch. XVI, 70 ; Ch. XXX, 27 ; Ch. LXX, 29.

7. The word "Karkhana" during Sultanate was used for the production centre as well as god won where the different kinds of articles stored, not only the production centre as modern times see K.M. Ashraf, *Hindustan Ke Logon Ke Jiwan Ki Samajik Aur Arthik Peristhitiyan*, (Delhi, 1969, Hindi tr., pp. 129-40.

8. A.I. Khaldun, *Muqqadamaa*, Utter Pradesh, 1961, Hindi tr., p. 432.

9. See R.P. Tripathi, *Some Aspects of The Muslim Administration*, Allahabad, 1974, Ch. VII, pp.239-54.

10. K.P. Jaiswal, *Hindu Polity*, Bombay, 1955, p. 330.

11. P. Saran, *Studies in Medieval Indian History*, Delhi, 1951, p. 19.

12. Three types of peasants were First, *Khud Qashta*—one who used to cultivate his own land, second, *Pahi Qashata* one who used to cultivate his own land but was inhabited in another place and third, *Muqrri Qashta* was that type of peasants who had plenty of land but used to cultivate their lands on contract basis or with the help of slave peasants or semi-slaves.

13. V.S. Miser, *Vividh Chintamani*, Gaikwar Oriental series, p. 70.

14. Barani, *Tarikhi-i-Ferozshahi*, Calcutta, 1960-62, p. 314.

15. A. Khusrau, *Izaj-i-Khusrawi*, Lucknow, 1875, Vol. IV, p. 206.

16. Barani, *op. cit.*, p. 314.

17. Minhaj, *Tabagat-i-Nasiri*, Calcutta, 1873-81, p. 168.

18. A. Khusrau, *op. cit.*, p. 334.

19. A.G. Shirf, (ed.), *Padmavat*, pp. 322-23.

20. Maulana Noor Turk was famous Sufi of 13th century. He was a bitter critics of Ulema-i-Duniyabi.
21. A. Hasan Sijji, "Fawaid-ul-Fawuid, p. 199, "Ab da Gulami Budnwa Andrf Har Roj Yek Dirham, Thma Maulana Bdari Wajah mash Va Hma Badrsta".
22. M.H. Kalander, *Khair-ul-Majalis*, Aligarh, p. 88.
23. Officer of Kitchen.
24. Officer of Drinks.
25. Officer of Sultan's Bathing, Clothing and Dressing.
26. Barani, *op. cit.*, p. 245.
27. Batuttah, *Rehla*, (ed. by A.M. Husin, Gaikwar Oriental Seirs), p. 105.
28. Afif, *Tarikh-i-Ferozshahi*, Calcutta, 1980, p. 270.
29. *Ibid.*, p. 269.
30. A. Khusrau, *op. cit.*, Vol. IV, p. 87-89.
31. For detail see A.B.M. Habibullah, *Foundation of Muslim Rule in India*, Allahabad, 1976, pp. 51-64.
32. For detail see *Ibid.*, pp. 96-115, Minhaj, *op. cit.*, pp. 165-228, Isamt, *Futuh-us-Salatin*, Madra, 1948, pp. 129-63.
33. For detail see Minhaj, *op. cit.*, pp. 281-360, *Ibid.*, pp. 108-63.
34. Afif, *op. cit.*, p. 436.
35. Yahya, *Tarikh-i-Mubarakshashi*, (Basu text), pp. 144-47.
36. Barani, *op. cit.*, p. 157.
37. Batutta, *op. cit.*, p. XXV.
38. Afif, *op. cit.*, pp. 270-73.
39. K.M. Ashraf, *op. cit.*, p. 129.
40. For detail see Barani, *op. cit.*, pp. 303-19, A. Khusrau, *Khazain-ul-Futuh*, Aligarh, 1924, pp. 15-17, Ferishta, *Tarikh-i-Ferishta*, Lucknow, pp. 114-17.
41. A. Khusrau, *Ibid.*, p. 13.

42. Skilled workers of Professional workers.

43. The right of land of the peasants had recognition. Peasants used to cultivate the land and were paying the fixed portion of crops as a revenue to the state. W.H. Moreland writes "Peasants feed up the Sultan's valley by paying revenue. Sultans were oftenly remains busy in punitive expeditions against the rebellious Subedars and nobility. In this way peasant's duty only was the payment of revenue to the state they were not told what was the demand, how it was assessed or in what form it was collected. *The Agrarian System of Moslem India*, Allahabad, 1963, Hindi tr., p. 41.

44. e.g., Balban had fixed 1/3 of produce, Alauddin Khalji had fixed 1/2 of the produce where as Ferozshah had fixed 1/5 of the produce as a 'Kharaj' or state share.

45. e.g., Blacksmith, Barber, Washerman, Cobbler, Weaver, etc.

46. Afif, *op. cit.*, p. 180.

47. Barani, *op. cit.*, p. 473.

48. N. Muh, Aufi, *Jawami-ul-Hikayat*, p. 105.

49. Afif, *op. cit.*, p. 269.

50. Anonymous, *Fiqa-i-Ferozshahi*, p. 186.

51. R. Mushtaqi, *Waqiat-i-Mushtaqi*, f. 802 b.

52. Barani, *op. cit.*, p. 40.

53. *Ibid.*, pp. 40-41.

54. Balban showed his ability and Sultan Iltutmish appointed him as *Khasadar*, Minhaj, *op. cit.*, p. 282.

55. Shiha-al-Din-al-Umari, *Masalik-al-absar-fi-Mamalik-al-Amsar*, S.A.A. Rizbi, hindi tr., Aligarh, 1956, p. 316.

56. Multan, Hisar-Feroza, Samana, etc., Afif, *op. cit.*, p. 270.

57. *Ibid.*, p. 268-73.

58. K.M. Ashraf, *op. cit.*, p. 139.

59. Barani, *op. cit.*, p. 554.

60. K.M. Ashraf, *op. cit.*, p. 124.
61. Barani, *op. cit.*, p. 100, W.H. Moreland, *op. cit.*, p. 45.
62. *Ibid.*, p. 228.
63. *Ibid.*, p. 429.
64. Department of Agriculture.
65. *Ibid.*, p. 498.
66. Provinces were divided into "Shiqs" to avoid the burden of administration and its officer was called as "Shiqdar".
67. *Ibid.*, p. 574.
68. Afif, *op. cit.*, p. 180.
69. R. Mushtaqi, *op. cit.*, f. 82 b.
70. Abdullah, *Tarikh-i-Daudi*, Aligarh, 1954, p. 36.
71. A. Khan Sharwani, *Tarikh-i-Shershahi*, p. 22.
72. Afif, *op. cit.*, pp. 112, 289, Shrafuddin Yazdi, *Zafar Namah*, Pt. II, pp. 87, 152.
73. A. Khusrau, *Kuliyat-i-Khusrawi*, pp. 204-05.

3

Role of Qazi During Delhi Sultanate

The justice is one of the most important piller of the sound administration. The administration of justice in Islam is administered in the name of God, not in the name of Caliph or Sultan because equality is the fundamental principle of Muslim legal and social code. All muslims are equal before the God, who is the suprem head, the only sovereign, ruling over men, through his messangers and revealed book.[1] *Quran* says, "Obey God, the Prophet and one who rules over you." Islam possesses neither Church nor priest nor a temporal power (king). Man must address God directly without seeking any mediator and the judge must give judgement according to the Will of God as stated in Quran. Therefore, it is administered with the reference to the Laws of *Quran*, *Hadis*, *Ijma* and *Qiyas*. Theoretically, in Islamic state it was the duty of Caliph as the successor of Prophet Mohammed.

In the beginning, Caliph was responsible for the *Qaza* or Judicial Administration. This tradition continued to the 14th Abbasi Caliph named Muhatdi Abbasi.[2] He was supposed to delegate his powers to the rulers of different states, who appointed the Qazis to assist them in Judicial administration by their knowledge of Muslim Law or *Sara*. As our historian Barani rightly remarked that, "Justice is that balance in which the good and bad deeds of men weighted".[3]

The founder of the judiciary in Islam was the Holy Prophet but Hazarat Umar was the first to established the judiciary as an institution seperate from the administration.[4] Whose legal formulation of the Muslim Polity was the "Shara" which was above the ruler and ruled. Thus the low and high were equal while appearing before the bar of "Shara".

In the middle Ages the department of justice was known as the *Diwan-i-Qaza* which was related to the department of *Siyasat* and *Mazalim* or grievances but it was mainly concerned with the civil litigations.[5] *Qaza* is a plural of *Aiqziyah*, a Arabic word which means consummating[6] or to give judgement in the controversies and in settling disputes.[7] *Diwan-i-Qaza* was the name of his office or department of justice.

Qazi-i-Mamalik was the Chief Judge of the Empire his court was the highest court of justice during the Caliphate. But during the Delhi Sultanate his court was next to the Sultan's Court. His subordinate official was *Naib-i-Qaza* who helped the chief Qazi to perform his functions. There were some *mufti* who interpret the *Shariat* and give their expert suggestions to the Qazi or ruler in the litigations; *Khatib* was the recorder of the court. There were also the officials such as *Amir-i-Dad*, *Kotwal*, *muhtasib*, etc., who help the Qazi. But in these papers, it is difficult to describe about them. We are bound to our limited subject, *i e.*, Role of Qazi.

Caliph Harun Rashid had established the court of *Diwan-i-Qaza*, when Imam Abu Yusuf was appointed as the Chief Judge or *Qazi* of Baghdad.[8] During the Caliphate of *Amir-ul-Muminin* Umar, a letter to the Abu Musa Ashari, Government of the Iraq, wrote him to appoint judge in the lands.[9] Hence the office of the Qazi comes in a separate existence with a specified instructions, powers and jurisdiction.[10] Umar's letter contains such instructions that the future of the qazis office was assured and developable.

In theoretically, *Qazi* or judge was appointed by the Caliph but with the extent of empire he was supposed to delegate his

power to the rulers of different states.[11] Therefore, in practically *Qazi* was appointed by the ruler of the Muslim state with his (appointed qazi) consent,[12] Muslim Law is very much clear on the appointment of qazi that he should be adult, a free man, Muslim, same and unconvicted of slander.[13] With the course of time, sultan created the post of *Sheikh-ul-Islam*, who recommended the appointments of the suitable and efficient qazi. Another department was also developed by the Arabs known as *Nazar-ul-Mazalim*[14] which deal with those cases which were the miscarriage of justice. In this way Qazi had an unique place in *Qaza* or Judicial Administration.

Only sovereign ruler or his wazir can appoint the "Qazi" by his oral or written order subjected to the acceptance of the individual concerned.[15] It is important to know that a non-muslim ruler or wazir or a governor can also appoint a qazi to administer the "Shara" or Islamic Law. Such appointment is valid under the cannon-law of Islam or "Shara".[16]

Naib-Qazi could be appointed by the Qazi, if he was employed to do so, the death of the qazi did not effect the appointment of the *Naib-Qazi*.[17] In this way *Qazian* were appointed by the Caliph or ruler or *Wazir* after the death of Prophet Mohammed.[18] He was respected without any doubts by the Ulema and all the people of state.[19]

Islamic law had a well defined qualifications for the appointment of *Qazi*. According to *Hedaya*,[20] he must have all the qualifications of a witness. The first qualifications that he must be a male,[21] adult, mently and Physically sound, free citizen and muslim.[22] Moreover, he must be a person of good understanding and perception as well as having a sound eye-sight and hearing organs[23] and knowledge of *Shariat*.[24]

In the earlier chronicles, there were detailed accounts of the conduct of Qazi but a few reference were available during the period of our study. Qazi's conduct was required to be above all the suspicions. He would not accepts the gifts from the friends and relatives and invitation of any entertainment except

of a general nature. Further he should not entertain any party with the other one.[25] He should not prompt or instruct a witness,[26] to show that he was favouring one or other party or in other words that his behaviour should be impartial to the both parties of a litigation. However, he was entitled to compell the defendant or *Mudda'i-illah* to appear before the law, just to meet the requirements of law or grant bail to him. It seems that to help the defendant was perfectly lawful.[27]

In the early medieval period, qazi used to hold his court in a Mosque.[28] But during Delhi Sultanate Sultan was the main source of justice, who used to sit in the court. After his court *Diwan-i-Qaza* was the important court, whose official was *Qazi-i-Mamalik* or *Qazi-ul-quzat* or *Sadr-i-Jahan*. He used to decide the cases in the open court in front of the public or used to sit in the court at a such place where sultan could not see him.[29] Shihabuddin-al-Umari enriches our knowledge with the account that "Only *Khans*, *Sadr-i-Jahan* and *Dabir* can sit in front of the sultan".[30] During the reign of sultan Ferozshah Tughluq, *Qazi-i-Mamalik*, *Sadr-i-Jahan* used to sit in the right hand side of the throne between the *Wazir-i-Mamalik*".[31] In the reign of Ibrahim Lodi, Qazi used to sit on the silver chair.[32]

In the court of Qazi there will be *Muftis* and *Ulamas* on the right and left side of the Qazi's seat or chair. In front of his chair or seat, there were *Khatib* or *Amin* (Clerk) of the court. There was a table in front of Qazi which was covered with a coloured cloth. The *Muhajir* and *Sijilat* or records file were kept on his table. There were also two parties sitting on the ground in front of him.[33] In the end of the hall, there would sit the witnesses and the partisians of litigants". *Daroga-i-Adalat* placed before him the important files and documents of the litigations. In this way court of Qazi forms the normal organ of the administration of law and the pivot of the judicial system.[34]

Contemporary or later chroniclers of Delhi sultanate, did not write about the fees of the Qazi's court. But it was certain

that qazi were paid by the plaintiff or probably by the defendant at any rate or by the successful party. It was confirmed by the law books that he was paid from the public treasury or *Bait-ul-Mal* because he performed the public works.[35] Abu Yusuf, further clears that fees was not legally payable by the litigants.[36] But we don't have such accounts during the period of our study. People paying the taxes such as *Dadbegi*, *Kotwali*, *Ihtsabi*, etc., and these taxes were credited to the Bait-ul-Mal[37] possibly, there was no fees for the registration of suits or cases in the court.

Qazi used to hear and decide all the disputes or cases relating to Civil, or Criminal and Religious nature. The proceeding of his court was simple, who suits the case or claims in the court was called *Plaintiff* or *Mudai* and who defends the case or against whom the claims demanded was called "Defendant" or *Mudda-i-illah*". "Plantiff" or *Mudai* go to the court with a written or oral application. "Khatib" or "Amin" of the court write his claim in word by word, neither should he add nor omite a single word.[38] They should also note the date of the claim. *Daroga-i-Adalat* brings the record file and related documents to the Qazi. The "Plantiff" or *Mudai* goes to near the *Khatib* and put his hand over the suit papers or read out the facts of his claim and he writes the suit on the court's register. If the claim is false, he should tell him that his claim is false.

In the court, Qazi must accord equal treatment to the both parties in hearing and entering. Both the parties and witnesses[39] made their statement without adding or omitting any word in the claim of claimant or denial defendant, If the law was not clear on any point of suit or case, he can consult the *muftis*. In the judgement, he was guided by the equity, common sense and precedents.[40] If there were a number of litigants, he must begin with first come or arrived at the same time.[41]

Qazi had to decide the litigations or cases according to *Shara* and *Hadis* or in accordance with 'Equity' or *Ijma* and reason depending on 'Analogy' or *Qiyas*. He should not

deliver his judgement in the presence of the witness and without the consultation of *muftis* if the claim of claimant was not clear. Neither he threats any body nor dectate. Unfortunately, we are unable to trace the narration of the proceedings of the Qazi's court. How the claims of claimant was decided? Possibly, there was a no change in courts works process. Claimant can claim his rights by a written or oral petition. Only Umari writes that, "If any desired to request the sultan or he can delay until needy person furnishes his request or complaint".[42]

Now the question arises to discuss that how much salary was received by the Qazi? During the early period (Caliph Umar) he was paid 100 *Dirhams*[43] from the state treasury or *Bait-ul-Mal*[44], but during the caliphate of Abu Mamun, Qazi received 400 *dirhams* per month.[45] During Delhi Sultanate Qazi was sufficiently paid to maintain his social status. Umari writes that *Qazi-ul-Quzat* was paid 60,000 *tankas* per year.[46] Ibn-i-Batutta increases our knowledge that when he was appointed as the qazi of Delhi. He was paid 12,000 *Dinars* per year.[47] On the other hand, there is also an account of less paid Qazi,[48] who used to take something from the both parties of litigation.

The tannure of the Qaziship was also not clear and certain in the sources. But from the analytically study of the sources, we can conclude that Quazi remains in his office till sultan or ruler had a good faith in him. During the early period of our study, death of ruler does not terminate the services of Qazi.[49] But during Delhi Sultanate every new sultan appointed a new Chief-Justice or *Qazi-i-Mamalik*, he can remove him from his office—at any time.[50] His dismissal or removal must be announced publically because public must know the facts for which he was dismissed.[51]

Further the question arises that what was the jurisdiction of qazi? With the help of his jurisdiction we are able to decide his status. The powers of jurisdiction of the modern judges and courts are specified by the legislation, but the Islamic courts were more or less depended upon opinion of the sovereign and

jurists. So far in general R. Levy rightly says that, "Judging the persons accused and allotting punishment is the function of quazi".[52] In fact the jurisdiction of qazi was only those matters which were referred to him which were popularly connected with religion such as marriage and divorce, inheritance and *Waqf* (pious foundation) and others matter had nearly always came before the lay authority who decided not only recording to *Fiqh*[53] but also according to the *Ada* which was a customary-law deffering from place to place.[54]

The first duty of Qazi was to take all the previous documents from the former qazi and fully checked them with the help of *Amins* or *Khatib*. He should get separately all the files from the former qazi, make a enquiry about the imprisoned political prisioners and re-investigate their cases.[55] Even in theory the qazi was not concerned with any thing beyond making all executive functions of the law being left to the *Amir* or the secular rules.[56]

In the beginning of Muslim Kingdom, the function of qazi was to decide the disputes of all types, to hear the appeals against the lower courts, to decide the provincial disputes which were referred to him, etc., according to the *Quran*, *Hadis*, *Ijma* and *Qiyas* but his decisions should not be against any customary law.[57] With the extent of Caliphate, his jurisdiction was considerably increased and embraced the supervision and management of the property of orphans and lunatics,[58] the execution of testamentary, disposition, the supervision of *Waqf*. Even he helps destitute widows to find suitable husband to them.[59]

Qazi was also responsible for the maintenance of streets and cities such as the prevention of encroachment in public through fares or an open spaces. He also supervised the working of all other lower courts and subordinate courts of the realm and above all to act as a legal adviser to the sultan. Where there was no other separate officer to collect the *Sadqat*, he had to collect the tax in those regions.[60] He was the protector of the people's rights.[61] But he can give his decision only when

defendant or "Muddaq-i-illah" accepts his crime but on his refusal he cannot give his decision. Further Abbasid Caliphs were not ready to allow independence to the courts. Therefore, the premptory directions were issued by the ruler to the judiciary or reversal of their decisions and arbitrary dismissal of those who had incurred the displeasure of their masters.[62]

During Delhi Sultanate, we finds that some times qazi was offered with the office of *Sadr-i-Jahan*,[63] *Khitabat* and *Imamat*.[64] These officials comes under the jurisdiction of *Diwan-i-Risalat*, which deal with the ecclisiatical affairs of the realm. So we can say that qazi had to supervise the works of "*Diwan-i-Risalat*". He had to also look after the management of *Madarsas*, accounts of the stipend granted to scholars, religious people or saints, sufis or *Darveshes* and needy people, etc.[65]

If his jurisdiction was general, it comprises the setting of dispute either by arbitration on lawful terms between the both parties or by enforcing liabilities by his verdiction in favour of those entitled upon disputed persons but only after having proofs which may be either by the permission of law or by evidences.[66]

If a qazi was not efficient in jurisprudence or feels indifferent in applying the law to a point of dispute, he was entitled to consult a competent jurists or *Muftis*. Those were suppose to help him in judicial matters. If he does not agree with the *muftis* views or Law was ambiguous or silent on any particular point such dispute was referred to the ruler or Sultan.[67] If qazi was well versed in jurisprudence and capable of making analogical deductions or *ijtihad*, he may draw his own conclusions and applying the results to the facts and circumstances of those cases and delivered his judgement accordingly.

Inspite of this, he had to keep in view the directives of the rulers because qazi was subordinate of the ruler or Sultan. So he was bound to the orders and decrees of the political authority and lower qazis by the higher qazis. But such directives issued to them, were essentially administrative nature......in addition there were several recorded instances of the judges or

qazis, those were seeking and receiving the advices of their political authority on the some points of law.[68]

Parallel to this, during Delhi Sultanate qazi always keeps in view their position, monetary as well as earning interest and delivered their decision.[69] In fact qazi exercise the authority in all illegal matters in theory but he was an authority in practical who decided disputes and to whom persons aggrieved themselves incapable to exacting it.[70]

In this way, qazi had a great limitation in itself such as *Qazi-i-Mamalik* or Chief Judge was appointed by the Sultan in good faith of the political authority, whereas the qazis of different provinces, and towns were appointed by the *Qazi-ul-Quzat* or *Qazi-i-Mamalik* but they continued to work untill they failed to get the favour and confidence of sultan. We are able to trace the such examples that with the change of sultan, qazi was also changed.[71] Although, qazi deal with the claims against high authorities of state such as sultan.[72] But it was simply the result of qazi to be enforce them by the machinery at his command.[73]

On one hand, *Qazi-ul-Quzat* decided the local disputes and litigations, on other hand, he hear the appeals against the lower courts. According to Muslim Law, the qazi or the judge has power to hear appeal both on fact and law. But it appears from the observations of certain jurists that the qazi of a higher-court can revise the decisions of a lower court on a point of law also.[74]

Although, Qazi decided the both type or Civil and Criminal cases of the people and hears the appeal against the judgement of lower courts. He decided the litigations of muslims in accordance to *Shariat* but civil disputes among the non-Muslims were decided by their own non-Muslims Judges or 'Panchayat'. While the disputes between non-Muslims and Muslims were decided by qazi or Muslim-judges according to the Muslim-laws or *Shariat*. Barani, who had too much prejudice against non-Muslims, narrated that, "Sultan Feroz-shah Tughluq offer them a choice relating to Shara.[75] Minhaj

also narrates regarding the works of qazi that, "Main function of qazi was to decide the people's disputes and give them protection from the tyrants".[76]

In the political matters, he was authorised to exercise the law of *Shara*. He can issues a decree or *Fatwa* against the works of Sultan.[77] Although he was appointed by the sultan but at the time of accession, qazi served the *Coronation-Oath*.[78] He also assist the Sultan in the appointments of different qazis.[79] During Tughluq Sultanate, the dead body of a traveller was not burried without the qazis seal and signature on the report.[80]

During the Sultanate *Qazi i-Mamalik* and *Qazi* of the city outworthy, appears to be politicians but could not successfull in their political greed, and severely published by the sultan.[81] Qazi was appointed as a envoy to the other sultans or States. Some times he was assigned to sign a treaty between two groups of nobles.[82] He also had some suggestive functions in regarding the religious, social and administrative policy. But he has not compelled to agree with his suggestions. Sultan followed their suggestions according to the circumstances.[83] He was also act as a legal adviser to the Sultan.[84]

As a whole, Qazi was heared the cases and administered the law and religious as well as performed the administrative, suggestive, diplomatic functions. His jurisdiction also exiended to the military functions during the Sultanate.[85] His jurisdiction was specified by the appointment-letter for example *Qazi-i-Mamalik* or *Qazi-ul-Quzat* was the chief justice of the Sultanate and was responsible for the administration of justice.[86] This rank was offered during al-Mahdi's Caliphate.[87] Similarly *Qazi-i Lashkar* was responsible for the administration of justice in military and declared the Sultan's decrees.[88]

Now we come to next point that jurisdiction of Qazi had any limitation? From the above discussion, positively, we can say that yes, there were some limitations on the Qazi's jurisdiction. We know that qazi was appointed by the Sultan or Ruler, the tenure of his office depends upon the discreation of Sultan. Hence he was not free to do whatever he likes.

Law or *Shariat* was the first limitation. He has to follow the "Sbara" in deciding the dispute cannot act contrary to the costumary laws laid by a clear text of "Quran" or of a universally accepted or well known tradition, *i.e.*, *Hadis* or by the consensus of opinion or *Ijma*. A subject to the restriction in stated that, "a qazee is free to make his own deduction in the matter of juristic law and may decide a suit on analogical deductions in the consonnance with the principles of "Equity and Justice.[89]

The procedure of current was also a restriction on the qazi. As in civil litigation qazi was first resort the parties coming before him and their suit orally or written to the *Amin* or *Khatib* of the court. The strict rules of procedure are enumerated by the law books before the trial of disputes for him.[90] In theory the decisions of qazi, however reached, was final and no appeal could be made.[91] But in practice he might be compelled to reverse his decision by the governor and successor of an unjust qazi can be reversed his decision.[92] During Delhi Sultanate we knows that Sultan appointed qazis of the different parts of the Sultanate, by the suggestion of *Qazi-i-Mamalik*. Therefore, they were independent from the influence of "Subedars" or Governors. There may be no logic to change their decision, even a few qazis does not fear from the Sultan.[93]

In this way court of qazi was the pivot of Judicial administration whereas judicial system was the pivot of sound administration. Therefore, just to established the sound administration, to run impartial justice, judiciary must be well organised. In Delhi Sultanate, we had different types of qazis such as *Qazi-i-Mamalik*.[94] *Qazi-ul-Quzat*[95], *Qazi*[96], *Naib-Qazi*[97], etc., who were appointed by the Sultan with the consent of *Qazi-i-Mamalik* or *Qazi-ul-Qazat*. They were completely free from the influence of Governors.[98]

Qazi-i-Mamalik or *Qazi-ul-Qazat* was the highest judicial authority next to the Sultan, was responsible for the smooth working of the judiciary. Generally, Sultan appointed the *Qazian* or Judges of the different provinces towns on his consent. He was a Chief Judge may be resided in provincial

capital or appointed to the important provinces. The maximum, Sultans of Delhi Sultanate appointed. *Qazi-ul-Quzat* only at Delhi, but during the Tughluq Sultanate *Qazi-ul-Quzat* was also appointed at in Daultabad.[99] It seems that Sultans cautious to set up a sound judicial administration only in the capital. Any how, we neither fully blamed the Sultan nor fully spare for this. Generally the contemporary Chroniclers does not deal with judicial system of that time.

Qazi-i-Lashkar was appointed in the military who was responsible for the judicial system in military or decided the cases among soldiers. He exercised a extent of influence over sultan such as during the reign of Sultan Giyasuddin Balban he was entitled with the title of *Harman.*[100] He used to declared the new *Farmans* or decrees of Sultan.[101] It may be added that his influence over Sultan that *Qazi-i-Lashkar* who fear from the God but not the Sultan, was respected by Sultan Balban and his recommendations were honoured by him.[103]

There were number of qazis appointed in the empire. As a whole, we are able to trace the 182 names of different Qazi's appointed in the different region of the Sultanate. The works of qaza and Eccliastical affairs or office of *Qazi-i-Mamalik* and *Sadr-i-Jahan* were offered to one person who was responsible for the judicial as well as religious functions.

During the Delhi Sultanate the works of qazi were also increased, so he had *Naib-Qazi* who helped him and also responsible for the administration of justice in the absence of the qazi.[103] There is also a reference of date *Hajib-i-Qazian*[104], but unfortunately, we are unable to trace the accounts of his duties. Perhaps, he may be the *Hajib* of *Qazi*. There is also a reference of *Qazi-i-Shah* but no account of his duties available. Perhaps, he may be the senior qazi of a big city. We also observed that there was a *Dar-ul-Qaza* in every town.

In the Sultanate, qazi had to settle the civil disputes as well as the many other works such as management of *Madarsa*, *Tazkir*, *Khitabat*, *Imamat*, etc.[105] Some of the qazis were essentially politicians in their outlook such as conversation

between the Sultan Alauddin and Qazi Mugisuddin of Bayana,[106] Sultan Jalaluddin Khalji suggested his wife[107] that whenever *Qazi* and *Sadr* comes to his palace, tell them that they advice the Sultan that he should entitled himself the title of *Al-Mujahid-fi-S'bi-a-Illah*,[108] Qazi Jalaluddin Kashani joined the conspiracy of Siddi Maula and severely punished.[109] K.A. Nizami has rightly observed that, "Qazi were politicians in their out-look but could not raise above the mad race for political power which had became a feature of this age......"[110]

Qazi also performed the deplomatic functions such as Sultan Alauddin Masud Shah send Qazi Jalaluddin Kashni of Awadh to Lakhnauti with *Chattar* and *Khilat*.[111] Similarly Sultan zain feroz send a group of envoy to the Shah Hasan of Sind among them qazi was also a member of the Envoy group.[113]

Qazi-Sadr-i-Jahan used to decide the Civil cases as well as he had to performed the religious functions such as distribution of prizes or *Idars* to the scholars and religious persons which were the duties of *Sadr-i-Jahan* during the Mughals. On the point Barani rightly narrates that all these duties included in the *Dar-ul-Qaza*.[113] In the provinces the judicial as well as eccliastical functions was performed by the qazi.[114] We agree with the Barani's reference because in some provinces we are able to find the post of 'Sadr'.

During Delhi Sultanate the office of qazi was regularly influenced with the change of Sultan. Every new Sultan appointed a new qazi. From which, we can conclude that the 'Qazi' of Sultanate was different to those of Early Medieval "Qazi". On the same way with the change of a influential noble the qaza was also effected such as Imaduddin Rehan terminated the Minhaj and appointed a new *Qazi-i-Mamalik*.[115]

Office of the qaza during the Sultanage attained a new feature of hereditory nature. Because we are able to traced such examples where the office of Qazi was offered to the decreased qazi's son.[116] Possibly the office of the Qaza in provinces will had been gained such hereditory nature.

In the beginning of the Sultanate, *Qazi-ul-Quzat* used to sit as a court of first instance in Delhi but with the course of time a separate qazi was appointed at the Capital.[117] The justice imparted in the court of qazi was simple, cheap and tough and apt of miscarries such as qazi trying to direct the defendant.[118] But he was free to verdict his decision to the every body.[119] Besides judicial and eccliastical and administrative function, qazi was also act as a legal advisor to the Sultan.[120]

Hence, we can conclude as a whole that there were two types of qazi such as qazi with limited powers and qazi with unlimited powers. Qazi with unlimited powers had a jurisdiction over all the type of cases such as religious law, question of claims, right of heritance, succession and coronation-oath, matrimonial disputes, etc., where as the qazi with limited powers had a limited jurisdiction according to his appointment letter.

During Delhi Sultanate there was four types of qazi, *i.e.*, *Qazi-i-Mamalik* or *Qazi-i-Mamalik*, *Sadr-i-Jahan*, and *Qazi-ul-Quzat* and *Qazi-i-Lashkar* whose jurisdiction were limited according to their appointments letter.

Unfortunately, that we don't have any information regarding the functions of *Qazi-i-Shah*, *Hajib-i-Qazian* and *Qazi-Khan*. But we can guess merely that perhaps *Qazi-i-Shah* may be the senior qazi of a town or provinces or may be the head of the city's qazis. Different sultans of Delhi had a different number of qazi in the capital such as Sultan Balban and Sultan Alauddin Khalji had three qazi of different qualifications.[121]

At least but not last that qazi was guided by the Quaranic text, public opinion (*Rai Akhbar*) discreation (*Darayat*) and integrity. But during Delhi Sultanate, Qazi's decisions were effected by the secular ambitions they actively participated in political affairs but could not be successful in attaining their objects. His office was equally effected with change of sultan as well as with the change of important nobles of the court, hence he tried to attain the political colour but fail to coloured himself.

REFERENCES

1. Mawardi, *Ahkam-i-Sultanayh*, Karachi, n. d., p. 186, A.M.A. Shushtery, *Outlines of Islamic Culture*, Banglore, 1938, Vol. II, p. 623.
2. I. Khaldun, *Muqqadamma*, Uttar Pradesh, 1961, Hindi tr. by S.A.A. Rizvi, p. 225.
3. Barani, *Fatawa-i-Jahandari*, eng. tr. by Afsar Begum, ed. by Moh. Habib, Allahabad, advice No. XV.
4. Mahmud-bin-Muhammad Arnuz, *Tarikh-ul-qaza-fil-Islam*, Lahore, 1960, p. 37, Khaldun, *op. cit.*, p. 225.
5. I.H. Qureshi, *The Administration of Delhi Sultanate*, New Delhi, 1971, p. 159.
6. T.P. Huges, *Dictionary of Islam*, Delhi, 1973, p. 479.
7. Moh. Aslam, *Muslim Conduct of State*, eng. tr. of the Isfani's *Suluk-ul-Muluk*, Islamabad, 1974, p. 107, Isfani gives seven meanings of *Qaza*.
8. W. Hussain, "*The Administration of Justice During the Muslim Rule*, Delhi, 1977, p. 169, Arnuz, *op. cit.*, p. 37, Relying on Khaldun's narration.
9. Moh. Aslam, *op. cit.*, p. 110.
10. K. Ahmad, *Hazrat Umar Ke Sarkari Khatut*, Delhi, 1959, pp. 296-98, Mawardi, *op. cit.*, pp. 25-30, A.A.A. Fyzee, *A Modern Approach to Islam*, Bombay, 1963, pp. 42-43, *Journal of Royal Asiatic Society*, 1910, pp. 307, 311-12.
11. Moh. Aslam, *op. cit.*, p. 115.
12. *Ibid.*, p. 116, Utter these words that, "I make you Qazi in such and such regions".
13. *Ibid.*, pp. 111-19, Mawardi, *op. cit.*, Hydrabad, ed. 1931, pp. 119-21.
14. Board for the Inspection of Grievences.
15. *Hedaya*, tr. by C. Hamilton, Vol. II, Ch. XX, p 334, Mawardi, *Ibid.*, pp. 123, 125, 134.

16. A. Rahim, *Principle of Mohammadan Jurisprudence*, London, 1911, p. 338.
17. *Ibid.*, p. 389, *Hedaya*, Vol. II, Ch. I, p. 342, Moh. Aslam, *op. cit.*, pp. 160-61.
18. Khaldun, *op. cit.*, p. 225.
19. R.B. Lewis, ed., *The World of Islam*, London, 1976, p. 37.
20. *Hedaya*, Vol. II, Ch. XX, p. 334, Moh. Aslam, *op. cit.*, pp. 132-38.
21. On this qualification there was a confussion—Abu Hanifa was liberal to some extent and said, "A woman could act as a judge but only in those cases in which her testimony was legally admissible P. Saran, *Mughalon Ka Prantiya Prashasan*, Hindi tr., Lucknow, 1970, p. 333, But Tabri was more liberal and writes that, "A woman could be appointed a judge without any restriction". Mawardi, *op, cit.*, p. 187, Mawardi, Hydrabad, ed., p. 117.
22. An infidal could be appointed as a Qazi but he could exercised his judicial authority over his co-religionist, cannot compell to accept his decision, See Mawardi, *op. cit.*, p. 188, Mawardi, *Ibid.*, p. 118.
23. *Ibid.*, pp. 107-09, Moh. Aslam, *op. cit.*, pp. 137-38.
24. *Ibid.*, pp. 187-89, *Ibid.*, pp. 117-19, *Hedaya*, Vol. II, Ch. XX, p. 344, T.P. Huges, *op. cit.*, p. 255.
25. *Ibid.*, p. 208, *Ibid.*, p. 134, *Ibid.*, Vol. II, Ch. XX, pp. 334, 337, Khaldun, *op. cit.*, pp. 223-24, N. Shibli, *Al-Farooq*, Vol. II, pp. 316-17, H.K. Sherwani, *Early Muslim Political Thought and Administration*, Delhi, 1976, pp. 88-89.
26. *Hedaya*, Vol. II, Ch. XX. p. 335.
27. *Ibid.*, p. 332.
28. Moh. Aslam, *op. cit.*, p. 138.
29. Umari, *Masalik-al-Afsar-fi-Mamalik-al-Amsar*, Aligarh, 1956, p. 328.

30. *Ibid.*, pp. 329-30.
31. Afif, *Tarikh-i-Ferozshahi*, Calcutta, 1892, p. 281.
32. Elliot and Dowson, *Bharat Ka Itihas*, Hindi tr., Agra, 1968, Vol. II, p. 217.
33. Moh. Aslam, *op. cit.*, p. 145.
34. N.J. Coulson, *A History of Islamic Law*, Edinburgh, 1964, p. 130.
35. Abu Yusuf, *Kitab-ul-Kharaj*, Balukh, 1303 A.H., p. 115, Mawardi, *op. cit.*, p. 208, S. Khuda Bakhsh, *Politics in Islam*, Delhi, 1975, p. 132, R. Levy, *The Social Structure of Islam*, Cambridge Uni. Press, 1957, p. 346.
36. *Ibid.*, p. 115, R. Levy, *Ibid.*, p. 346.
37. Ferozshah, *Futuhat-i-Ferozshahi*, Aligarh, 1954, p, 5.
38. Moh. Aslam, *op. cit.*, p. 147.
39. Witness were required when defendant denied the claims of claimant, *Ibid.*, p. 148.
40. M. Nizam, *The Life and Times of The Sultan Mahmud of Gazna*, Camb. University Press, 1931, p. 148.
41. R. Levy, *op. cit.*, p. 343.
42. Umari, *op. cit.*, pp. 329-30.
43. A gold coin, which was equal about to the 96 Barely.
44. Mawardi, *op. cit.*, p. 208 ; Moh. Arnuz, *op. cit.*, p. 71, Moh. Aslam, *op. cit.*, p. 131.
45. *Suyuti-ul-Jalaluddin Hasan*, Ciaro, 1925, Vol. II, pp. 100, 101, 104, ascited by P.K. HiHi, "History of Arabs", New York, 1977, p. 326.
46. Umari, *op. cit.*, p. 317 ; Elliot & Dowson, *op. cit.*, Vol. III, p. 420.
47. Ibn-i-Batutta, *Rehla*, Paris, 1949, p. 402.
48. M.M. Bakkari, *Tarikh-i-Sind*, Bombay, 1938, p. 73.
49. Mawardi, *op. cit.*, pp. 125-35.

50. See the list of *Qazian During Delhi Sultanate*, Appendix-A.
51. W. Hussain, *op. cit.*, p. 160.
52. R. Levy, *op. cit.*, p. 338.
53. Law as elaborated by religious authorities.
54. *Ibid.*, p. 342 ; Khaldun, *op. cit.*, p. 224.
55. *Hedaya*, *op. cit.*, p. 336 ; Moh. Aslam, *op. cit.*, p. 138.
56. *Ibid.*, p. 378.
57. A. Rahim, *op. cit.*, p. 388.
58. R. Levy, *op. cit.*, p. 342.
59. Khaldun, *op. cit.*, p. 224.
60. Mawardi, *op. cit.*, p. 201.
61. Khaldun, *op. cit.*, p. 230.
62. N.J. Coulson, *op. cit.*, pp. 122, 123.
63. Barani, *Tarikh-i-Ferozshahi*, Catcutta, 1860-62, pp. 423, 428, 580, etc.
64. Minhaj, *Tabaqat-i-Nasiri*, Calcutta, 1873-81, pp. 175, 195, 249, 310, Amir Khurd, *Siyar-ul-Auliya*, Delhi, 1885, p. 84.
65. Barani, *Ibid.*, p. 580.
66. Khaldun, *op. cit.*, 223.
67. A.M. Hussain, *The Rise and Fall of Muhammad-bin-Tughluq*, Delhi, 1972, p. 222.
68. N.J. Coulson, *op. cit.*, pp. 29, 30 ; Barani, *op. cit.*, pp. 348, 352, 406.
69. *e.g.*—Qazi showed partiality to Sultan Muhammad-bin-Tughluq. See—Batuta, *op. cit.*, pp. 285-86.
70. R. Levy, *op. cit.*, p. 338.
71. *e.g.* See—Minhaj, *op. cit.*, pp. 195, 217, 218, 220, 228, 229, 303 ; Barani, *op. cit.*, pp. 210, 221, 222, etc., Yahya, *Tarikh-i-Mubarakshashi*, Calcutta, 1931, p. 358, etc. See also appendix—A.

72. Batutta, *op. cit.*, pp. 285-86.

73. N.J. Coulson, *op. cit.*, pp. 121-22, A. Khusrau, *Ijaz-i-Khusrawi*, Lucknow, 1875, Vol. II, p. 13, Hamiduddin Nagori, *Saroor-us-Sudoor*, Aligarh, pp. 44, 48.

74. Khaldun, *op. cit.*, p. 223, W. Husain, *op. cit.*, p. 73, Mohamed Ullah, *The Administration of Justice of Muslim Law*, Delhi, 1977, p. 67.

75. Barani, *op. cit.*, p. 580.

76. Minhaj, *op. cit.*, p. 195.

77. A. Khusrau, *op. cit.*, Vol. II, pp. 4-17.

78. Barani, *op. cit.*, p. 246, Yahya, *op. cit.*, p. 155, etc.

79. A. Khusrau, *op. cit.*, Vol. II, p. 13.

80. Yahya, *op. cit.*, pp. 140-41, Elliot & Dowson, *op. cit.*, Vol. IV, p. 14.

81. *e.g.*—Minhaj, *op. cit.*, pp. 193-94, 213, Barani, *op. cit.*, pp. 196-97, 210-11, Amir Khurd, *op. cit.*, p. 527.

82. *Ibid.*, pp. 188, 199, 302, *Ibid.*, p. 103, *Ibid.*, Vol. II, p. 249, Moh. Bakkari, *op. cit.*, p. 142.

83. Barani, *op. cit.*, pp. 196-97, 211, Abdullah, *Tarikh-i-Daudi*, Aligarh, 1954, pp. 29, 30, A. Yadgar, *Tarikh-i-Shahi*, Calcutta, 1939, pp. 30-31.

84. Afif. *op. cit.*, pp. 129, 130.

85. R. Mushtaqi, *Waqiyat-i-Mushtaqi*, Rotograph copy, Aligarh, p. 154.

86. A. Khusrau, *Khazain-ul-Futuh*, Aligarh, 1928, p. 7.

87. S.A.Q. Husaini, *Arab Administration*, Delhi, 1976, p. 167.

88. Afif, *op. cit.*, p. 378, Barani, *op. cit.*, pp. 47, 107, 108. Amir Hussan, Fawaid-ul-Fawud, Delhi, 1272 A.H., p. 232, Elliot & Dawson, *op. cit.*, Vol. III, p. 83.

89. Abdul S. Nadvi, *Al-Qaza-fil-Islam*, Lucknow, pp. 87-89, A. Rahim, *op. cit.*, p. 388, W. Hussain, *op. cit.*, p. 163.

90. Moh. Aslam, *op. cit.*, pp. 142-149, E. Levy, *op. cit.*, p. 343
91. *Ibid.*, p. 126.
92. R. Levy, *op. cit.*, p. 346.
93. We can cite an example of Balban's three Qazi. See—H. Nagori, *op. cit.*, pp. 47-48.
94. Chief Justice or Qazi of the empire.
95. Chief Judge of the empire.
96. Judges of the different areas such as town, village, etc.
97. Subordinate to the Qazi might be appointed in the important towns.
98. A. Khusrau, *Ijazi-i-Khusrawi*, Vol. II, p. 13, I.H. Qureshi, *op. cit.*, p. 161.
99. Sharf Jahan was appointed as a *Qazi-ul-Quzat*, at Daultabad, Batutta, *op. cit.*, p. 26.
100. "Harman" was a religious city of Makkah and Madina, Barani, *op. cit.*, p. 47.
101. Afif, *op. cit.*, p. 378.
102. Barani, *op. cit.*, p. 108.
103. When Minhaj was offered the "Qaza" of Gwalior, he was also responsible for the "Khitahat", "Ahtisab and Sarai" works. Sultan Raziya appointed him in Qaza of Gwalior and also appointed as a manager of "Madarsa-i-Nasiria" in Delhi, Minhaj, *op. cit.*, pp. 175, 188, 249.
104. Isami, *Futuh-us-Salatin*, Madras, 1948, p. 556.
105. Minhaj, *op. cit.*, pp. 124, 144, 175. 188, 200, 249, etc., Barani, *op. cit.*, pp. 290, 310.
106. Barani, *Ibid.*, pp. 290-96.
107. *Ibid.*, pp. 196-97.
108. Means fighter for God, *Ibid.*, p. 196.
109. *Ibid.*, p. 210.

110. K.A. Nizami, *Some Aspects of Religion and Politics During Thirteenth Century*, Aligarh, 1961, p. 166.
111. Minhaj, *op. cit.*, p. 199.
112. M. Bakkari, *op. cit.*, p. 142.
113. Barani, *op. cit.*, p. 380.
114. *Ibid.*, p. 423.
115. Minhaj, *op. cit.*, pp. 217, 220.
116. *Ibid.*, p. 226.
117. *Ibid.*, p. 220.
118. Batutta, *op. cit.*, pp. 280-81, Allauddin's Qazi's were like a puppat. See—Barani, *op. cit.*, pp. 351-52.
119. Barani, *Ibid.*, p. 40, Minhaj, *op. cit.*, p. 131, Abdullah, *op. cit.*, p. 131.
120. *Ibid.*, p. 353, Afif, *op. cit.*, pp. 129-30.
121. See—H. Nagori, *op. cit.*, pp. 47-48, Barani, *Ibid.*, pp. 351, 52.

4

Amir Khusrau As A Poet-Historian

Hazarat Amir Khusrau of Delhi is, no doubt, a heroic soul. Poet, writer, humorist, historian, soldier, courtier, mystic, musician and naturalist—he was all this. He was a profound humanist and in spite of his foreign origin[1] was a great lower of every thing Indian. He was a versatile man. He had seen the life from all angles, will all its turns and twists and lights and shades. Diversity was the essential nature of his life and nothing was too high or too low for him. The pomp and grandeur of the royal court, the state-finery of the market, the devoting and soothing atmosphere of the "Khanqah", he heard the din and clatter of arms in the war-fields, all these went to shaping his personality. The court and countryside, the monastery and the market place, the palaces of amirs, rulers and huts of the common people, all were equally important for him. In other words, he came in to a close and personal contact with kings and commoners, Sufis and soldiers, poets, scholars and musicians. In the long spane of his varied life he roamed in the Sultanate—from Delhi to Deogir, from Multan to Lakhnauti—and studied its flora and fauna, languages and customs. He witnessed the rise and fall of great dynasties and lived through the reigns of six sultans of Delhi Sultanate. In fact, very few men had such varied and close contact with so many facets of life as Amir Khusrau had.

A variety person Amir Khusrau was born in 651 A.H./1253

A.D. at Patiali, (Maminpura in Etah district of Uttar Pradesh) in the house of Amir Saifuddin Mahmud, a Turk of "Lachin tribe", at the time when Turks established the Chief governing class of Northern India. His mother was the daughter of Imadul-mulk, a reputed amir of Delhi. Amir Mahmud having determined to give his sons the full benefit of education. As he was a prosperous man[2] and could afford to arrange for the best means of instructing his children. Khusrau was sent to a "Maktab" at very early age and some scholars were engaged to teach him at home also. The bright boy made a rapid progress with his studies but he was a born poet and had inbibed an extra ordinary passion for poetry from his very cradle.

He writes (himself) about his early days, "My father used to send me to the 'maktab' for study but I repeated only rhymes, and my learned teacher—Saduddin Mohammad tried to teach me calligraphy, while I composed the verses about the silken down on fair faces".[3] In this way, he had passion for poetry right from the early age. Once his talent was tested by Khawaja Izzuddin with four discordant things namely—hair, egg., arrow and melon and told him to compose a quatrain in which these four words should occur. He composed, "Every hair in the tresses of that beauty has attached to it a thousand 'eggs', (*i.e.*, grains) of amber. But do not consider her nature to be straight as an arrow, for like the melon the teeth (*i.e.*, the seeds) are concealed within".[4] Khawaja Izzuddin was so much surprised at the genius of the youthful poet that he accorded him the designation of "Sultani-i-Shamsi" which is found in Amir Khusrau's earlier works.[5]

He was now firmly set on the path of poetry and he proceeded with vigour pace. But very soon, he had to face the first great despair of his life that his father thus left him an orphan of a eight years.[6] After death of his father Khusrau's maternal grandfather Imadul-Milk, who was "Rawat-Ard" for thirty years the one rousport of 'Ard-i-Mamalik', paid a special attention towards his education and training. The grandfather's attitude and the pure surroundings[7] heightened his innate faculties and God given natural aptitudes.

At an early age he became a youth of many parts obtaining high efficiency in the prevalent arts and literature, other branches of learning such as—Fiqh, astronomy, grammer, philosophy, logic, religion, mysticism, history and literature. Music also formed a part of his learning and he improved the prevalent art of music by his original contributions.[8] Even Sirajuddin Khan Arzu points out that those who have a cultivated ear and a knowledge of music can well appreciated the high quality of Amir Khusrau's couplets which not only expresses an appropriate sense in words, reproducing the sound of a drum but also pays full regard to the principles of musical harmony.[9]

In the field of language, he was the master of the Turkish, Persian and Arabic languages. He also learnt various Indian dialects especially Hindi that he loved too much and felt proud which shows from his couplits that :

A Turkish Indian, speaking Hindavi am I,

No lump of sugar or Arabic in expression.

Another couplet says—

Rightly speaking I am a 'Indian Finch',

Ask of me Hindavi that I may sing in it.

By this attitude he placed India above the rest of the world,[10] loved every particle and corner of India and called himself as a "Tuti-i-Hindavi".

Amir Khusrau was the most favourite deciple of Khawaja Nizamuddin Auliya. The Shaikh loved him so much that he had given him the pet name of "Turk-i-Allah" and usually addressed him. Similarly Khusrau had an unbounded love and devotion for his Spiritual Guru—Hazarat Nizamuddin Auliya and writes, "He is an emperor without a throne, without a crown but emperors stand in need of the dust of his feet". This was how, he described the greatness of his beloved spiritual Guru.

He was not only the mystic, musician, poet but also a courtier. He lived a long enough to see the reign of six Sultans and accession of seventh one,[11] who comming to throne and being murdered, dynasties being set up and pulled down. In other words, he witnessed the rise and fall of each king and each dynasty.[12] His intimate experience from Khanqah to Darbar and from the rendezvous of poets to the battle-fields sharpened him, deepened insight in the nature of man and things around.

Although, his maternal grand-father Imadul-Mulk was one of the reputed amirs of the Delhi Sultanate and held important offices like "Ard-i-Mamalik" and "Rawat-i-Ard". His death in 671 A.H./1272 A.D. lifted the umbrella of protection of the family. Amir Khusrau started trying his luck outside the bound of kingship. His career from the 20th year of his age can be summed up chronologically onwards that—in 671 A.H./ 1273 A.D. Khusrau joined the services in the court of the "Amir-i-Hajib" or the Chief-Chamberlain of the Sultanate, Alauddin Muhammed Kishli Khan, who commonly known by his nick name "Malik Chajju" was the nephew of Sultan Balban. He found in him an ideal hero—brave, chivalrous and generous that even Halaqu had offered him the governorship of half of the Iraq if he consented to join his services.[13] He served there for two years but after a trival incident[14] led to a serious misunderstanding and him to left his services.

Due to Bughra Khan, Khusrau had been dismissed by the Malik Chajju from his court. But we find that Amir Khusrau was soon in the service of Bughra Khan who was the governor of Samana at that time[15] and lived for some time when Tugharil Khan rose in rebellian at Lakhnauti in Bengal. Bughra Khan was summoned by his father Sultan Balban to suppress the revolt. He not only accompanied the prince to Lakhnauti but also drafted a "Fatah-Nama" to celebrate the success of compaign. He lived there unwillingly but the damp climate of Bengal did not suit him and he returned to Delhi probably in the year 679 A.H./1279 A.D.[16]

In Delhi, he met the Prince Muhammad, the eldest son of Sultan Balban who used to make yearly visit to his father with enormous gifts and presents from the Multan.[17] Prince took an instant liking for him and asked to accompany him to Multan. Khusrau took up service under him in 679 A.H./1280 A.D. and left for Multan. He lived at Multan for five years but his pleasant stay came to an abrupt end with the tragic death of Prince Muhammad, who lost his life in an encounter with Mongols.[18] He himself was captivated by the Mongols, any how he managed to escape.[19] He found himself deprived of a patron under whom his talent had been fully recognised and appreciated. He wrote a pathetic elegy mourning the death of Prince.

After the death of Prince, there was a brief gap in the service of Khusrau. Meanwhile he had attached himself to the brilliant Malik Amir Ali Sarjandar known as *Hatim Khan*, for his unbounded generosity. This pattern was a eminet Malik of Balban's court. When the *iqta* of Awadh was assigned to Amir Ali Sarjandar he took Khusrau along with him. He stayed in Awadh for about two years but all the time desired to return to Delhi. At last, he sought his patron's permission and came back again to Delhi which he loved very much.

Amir Khusrau, however, ignored and avoided the invitation of Sultan Muizzuddin Qaiqubad for some time. Hardly a couple of days had passed to his return to Delhi that a courtier from the court of Sultan Quiqubad brought an invitation for him.[21] He went to the court, recited a customary couplets in praise of the Sultan and was admitted among his courtiers. It was the Amir Khusrau's first appointment at the court of a Sultan of Delhi Sultanate.

Qaiqubad was a vicious and licentious, given to the pleasures of the body. During the reign Delhi turned into a haunt of pleasure and according to Barani, "Courtesans appeared in the shadow of every wall and beautiful women sunned themselves on every balcony. Not a street but sent forth a master of melody or a chanter of odes. Wine and women became the order of the day.[22] In the romantic atmosphere Khusrau appeared as a songster of Laura and Love. He produced his first historical poem *Qiran-us-Sadain*. In this historical poem he described the meeting of Sultan Muizzuddin Qaiqubad, the Sultan of Delhi with his father Nasiruddin Bughra Khan Governor of Bengal, by the bank of river Ghagra on one side and river Sarju on other side in Awadh in the year 688 A.H./1289 A.D. As this historical poem contains a penegyric on Delhi, some of its famous buildings, etc. He states that this historical poem was written by him in his 36th year of life and occupied for three months in writing. In contains 3,944 couplets.[24]

During the period of hectic political activity that preceded the rise of the Khaljis. The details about Khusrau's role are not available. When Jalaluddin Khalji the *Sarjandar* and governor of Samana came to Delhi and was appointed *Ariz-i-Mumalik*. He realized the way wind was blowing as his main principle of life—"was to keep pace with time" and joined his service. As Jalaluddin ascended the throne of Delhi, appointed the Khusrau as *Mushafalar*[25], admitted him into the circle of his *Nadims* and fixed an annual pension of 1200 *tankas*.[26]

Sultan was over seventy when he became the ruler of Delhi but his interest in life was as keen as ever. 'Each night' says Barani, "Amir Khusrau brought new Ghazals to the assembly of the king and while the *saqis* offered the forthing cups and beautiful damsels dances and sang, the ghazals of Amir Khusrau were recited. In those gathering which could scarcely be considered as of this earth, the lifeless ones got a fresh life and the sad hearts gladdened".[27] This is what Barani had to say of those days. He came closer to Sultan and became one of his most trusted *nadims*. He accompanied his patron when Malik Chajju, his former patron of Kara ross in rebellion.

During the reign of Jalaluddin Khali, in completed his fourth *Diwan-Ghurrat-ul-Kamal* historical poem *Miftah-ul-Futuh* is a historical sketch of the initial conquests of Jalaluddin Khalji in the year 690 A.H./1292 A.D.[28] In one *Qasida* he compares himself to *Khaqani* and Sultan to Khaqani's patron Jalaluddin *Akhtisun* Shirwan Shah.[29] He says, "May our Jalaluddin remain for ever at the head of our glorious kingdom and may his glorious deeds pass into history through our praise of them". But no sooner did Alauddin, murderer of his patron assend the throne he forget him. Khusrau congratulate the new Sultan with these words, May you be blassed with the glory of the *Khutba* of Delhi, this happy augury I draw from the mine lots of the Skies".[30]

Alauddin Khalji's accession gave a sense of security and stability to him. The twenty years of Alauddin's reign conincided with the most productive period of his life.[31] He completed his five romantic poems—*Matla-ul-Anwar*, *Shirin-o-Khusrau*, *Majnun-o-Laila*, *Aina-i-Sikandari*, *Hrsth-Bihisht* which are collectively known as *Panj Ganj* or *Khamsa-i-Khushrawi*. All these poems were dedicated to Shaikh Nizamuddin Auliya and presented to the Sultan Alauddin Khalji. But Sultan compelled him to stay at court and paid no regard to the honour due to such poet-historian and was content to give him his one thousand *tankas*.[32]

In spite of compulsion to stay at court the romatic poems would not be satisfied the Khusrau's passions, turned to prose and brought two works of different lengths. The first, *Khazain-ul-Futuh* is a thin volume on the history of Alauddin's campaigns—here Sultan has been praised for his successful military compaigns in the South, his effective grarrisoning of the North-Western Frontier and resistance against Mongol incursions. But successfully tried to hid the unsuccessful campaigns. His attempts at the reformation of public morals, his regulations against hoarders, profiteers, black marketers, the fraternity of incest, the prostitutes, magicians, etc. Second, *Ijaz-i-Khusrawi* is huge work in five volumes in figures of speech.

Towards the end of Alauddin's reign there came the best Khusrau's historical romantic poem, *Dewal Raniwa-Khizr Khan* with the course of events brought to the tragic conclusion. In this historical romantic poem he described the Alauddin's early campaigns and follows the conquest of Ranthambhore, captivity of Rai Karan's daughter Dewal Devi broughts to Sultan's haram, where the infact love grows between Khizr Khan and Dewal Devi, etc. In the end he supplemented about the crucification of Khizr Khan when the Mubarak Shah Khalji's reign came to an end.

After the death of Alauddin Khalji there was a brief interlude in which Malik Kafur and Sambul the two ennuchs exercised all the powers and eliminated the Alai nobles and princes from the positions of power but soon they were over throned by Qutabuddin Mubarak Shah Khalji as occupied the throne and Khusrau joined the court of Sultan Mubarak Khalji. Even he continued to stay at court when a conflict was taking place between Shaikh Nizamuddin Auliya and Sultan. He completed *Nuh-Sipihr* in the letter's reign. In which he pays an eloquent tribute to Sultan and says that the gifts he received from him were such that he had not obtained from any former rulers. He wrote at the instance of the Sultan. He has first praised his spiritual Guru and has turned towards the Sultan. This historical poem comprises 4509 couplets and deals with the various historical events of Sultan's reign. Third sipihr, contains an account of his own Indian descent and also an interesting account of the different language currently in the various parts of India. In the Ninth sipihr, he boasted his own command of language and characterisation of good poetry.

Ghiyasuddin Tughluq had great regard for Amir Khusrau and he joined his service soon after the accession. Khusrau greeted him enthusiastically. Tughluq Shah an extemely pious and virtuous man, soon won the heart of all his subject by his simplicity, sincerety and generousity and restored the order and peace throughout the dominions disturbed by the sad events at Delhi. Amir Khusrau seems to have accompanied the Prince Juna Khan, the eldest son of Sultan to Deogir in 722 A.H. and said to have drawn his attention to the beauties of the place[33] and possibilities of developing it as a Southern Capital.

Ghiyasuddin Tugluq treated Amir Khusrau very kindly and the poet was more prosperous in his reign then he had been before.[34] We wrote the historical poem *Tughlaq Namah* in which he described the conflict between *Parwaris* and the Ruler. In 724 A.H., he accompanied the Sultan on his Lakhnauti and Awadh campaigns. On his way back from Lakhnauti Sultan stayed for few hours at Afghanpur where the Prince Juna Khan had constructed a wooden pavillion for his reception. The structure suddenly collapsed and the Sultan was buried in the debris.

Amir Khusrau came back to Delhi with the army, a few months later to find that his Spiritual-Guru and patron-saint had also expired in the mean time. He store is clothes, put dust into his hairs and pathetically recited the verse :

"Gori soway sej per, Mukh per dare kes,
Chal Khusrau ghar aapane rain bhai chaudes."[35]

This shock was too great for him to bear and he spent few months in complete seclusion away from the court and camp, later he also died in 725 A.H./1325 A.D. and was buried at the foot of his Guru's grave.

In this way, Amir Khusrau had seen many changes and revolutions in the span of his life and from his grave he has seen many more. He was one of those lucky chroniclers who live long enough to see their fame spread far and wide, to have the satisfaction of their worth being recognised by their contemporaries and to be able to visualize the prospect of an ever increasing popularity and renown down in the depths of time among generations and nations yet unborn. Moreover, he had the good fortune of being able to collect and arrange the most of his works during the span of his life. As an officer and courtier he had to be a regular attendant at the court of his patrons some of whom, caring little, perhaps for poetry mere quite hard task-masters.

Further, he had an opportunities of witnessing the dazzle splendour of court life, the pomp and ceremonial connected with the accessions, coronations, and death of the successive rulers, peace and war, victory and defeat, success and failure, conquest and administration, marches and halts, change of government, tranquillity and tumult, luxury and pleasure, and munificence and generousity of the Rulers towards the men of note who gathered around the Imperial Court. Such scenes and surroundings could not fail to expert powerful influence on the mind of this "Lord of Language", "Lord of Descriptions", "First Medieval National Poet-Historian", and to act a "Whip to the steed" of his genius.

Amir Khusrau could not arrange all his works before his death in spite of all cares and labour.[36] Perhaps he had no time to arrange all his works. Barani the contemporary historian is vague on this issue.[37] According to Jami, the number of his works was ninety nine[38] and he has been followed by other biographers also.[39] Similarly Daulat Shah writer of *Tazkirat-ul-Shuara*", Amin Razi in his *Haft-Iqlim*, Ferishta in his *Tarikh-i-Ferishta* create a great confusion to the modern historians.

In 1915, the late Nawab Haj Mohammad Ishaq Khan tried to formed a project of editing and publishing the complete works of Amir Khusrau. He tried his best for discovering any works still unknown but able to trace only fourty five works.[40] But after some corrigendum[41] which eliminate sixteen of the eighteen works beginning from the No. twenty eight, thus we are left with only twenty nine works. Dr. Mohammad Wahid Mirza writes that there are only a list of twenty works of Amir Khusrau available in the different libraries[42] such as given below :

A. The five "Dewans"[43]—

1. "Tuhfat-us-Sighar" ; 2. "Wast-ul-Hayat" ;
3. "Ghurrat-ul-Kamal" ; 4. "Baqiya Nagiya" ;
5. "Nihayat-ul-Kamal".

B. The Historical Poems[44]—

1. "Qiran-us-Sadain" ; 2. "Miftah-ul-Futuh" ;

3. "Dewal Rani Khizr Khan" or "Ashiqa" or "Ishqia" ;
4. "Nuh Sipihr" ;
5. "Tughluq Namah".

C. The "Khamsa-i-Khusrawi"[45]—

1. "Matla-ul-Anwar" ;
2. "Shrin-o-Khusrau" ;
3. "Aina-i-Sikandari" ;
4. "Hasht-Bihisht" ;
5. "Majnun-o-Laila".

D. The "Gazliyat"—

Lyrical poems of Khusrau.[46]

E. Prose Works[47]—

1. The "Khazain-ul-Futuh" or "Tarikh-i-Alai" ;
2. "Afdal-ul-Fawaid" ;
3. "Ijaz-i-Khusrawi".

F. Hindi Poetry[48]—

The "Khaliq Bari" and other hindi poems ascribed to Khusrau.

In this way Amir Khusrau wrote so many books in poetry and prose but only twenty books are available in the different libraries. Our present effort is to evaluate Amir Khusrau as a Poet-Historian. As he had seen reign of six Sultans of Delhi and accession of seventh one and composed the poetry and prose in different works which are full of the factual information for the study of political, military and socio-economic condition of the contemporary and near-contemporary period.

First to evaluate his works we should like to discuss the main features of Medieval Historiography in India. Muslims had always a great sence of history and started composing works on Islam right from the day of Prophet Muhammad. Originally, these works were composed in Arabic, the language of *Qur'an*. But towards the close of tenth century Persian was adopted as substitute language. Consequently, when the

Turks came to India they brought with them the tradition of writing history in Persian. But the most of historians were connected with various kings and courts they indulged in panegyrics of their patron. Further most of these historians came from the Histocratic class, kept close to the rulers and ignored the life and conditions of the commoners. Third, they had a blind faith in the Superiority of Islam. For modern historians, to have a proper use of their works, it is necessary to have an idea about their cultural, social and religious background as well as their conception of history.

During the period of our study, Ziauddin Barani places the *History* on a equal footing with *Hadis.*[49] Where as our poet-historian was under scoring the charm of history on a aesthetic plane of poetry. Another light on Medieval view of history from our poet-historian's illustrious contemporary historian Barani, whose thought of history as a discipline which made men wise as they learnt from the experience of past.[50] Further more, prescribed that a historian should be honest and truthful and if one reason or the other his is unable to convey the facts, he should try.[51] Figures of speech stock rhetorical expressions and style of that era confused the modern historians. It is obvious that medieval historians understood their job as narrating and reporting of events that took place in the past or were taking place in their own time.

In evaluate the significance as well as historical importance of the works of Amir Khusrau it is necessary to have an idea about that period circumstances in which these were written or completed. In spite of all means and sources of information, why he tried to hid the events ? For example conspiracy of Siddi Maula during Sultan Jalaluddin Khalji, etc.

The chronology from 671 A.H. to 725 A.H./1273 to 1325 A.D. speaks volumes not of the variety of experiences. He was the contemporary of Sultan Balban to the Sultan Ghiyasuddin Tughluq. Because of the royal patronage, it was possible that he could not narrate such events which annoyed his patron or snatched his all means of livelihood. So he always tried to mention the purpose of his writings, *e.g.* In

Qiran-us-Sadain which was written at the request of Sultan Qaiqubad and was completed in 688 A.H. after the hard labour of three months[52] and was handsomely awarded by the ruler but eternal fame which was his only motive.[53] *Nuh sipihr* was composed to get the reward of gold equal to the weight of an elephant. Similarly his object of writing *Tughluq Namah* is clear that Khusrau with usual apologetic remarks about the quality of his work expresses the hope that it would gain renown by the auspicious approval of the king.[54]

Amir Khusrau was the contemporary courtier and chronicler of the Sultan Balban to the Sultan Ghiyasuddin Tughluq but not near-contemporary or later-chronicler.[55] The title of his works clearified the subject, *e.g.*, *Qiran-us-Sadain* means the conjunction of the two Auspicious stars ; *Miftah-ul-Futuh* means the keys to success or the early victories ; *Ashika* or *Ishqiya* means beloved or lovers : *Nuh sipihr* means the nine skies : *Tughluq Namah* means victory of Tughluq : Similarly *Khazain-ul-Futuh* means the treasury of victories.

Like the other chroniclers of Medieval Indian History, Amir Khusrau was also under the impact of Religion or Faith and mystic in sight. He begins his work with the praise of God and wishes the success of his patron by the grace of God and puts responsibility of failure of patron, prince on a "Divine Power or Fortune". On the other hand, for the success of each project of his patrons, believes in Divine Power, which was the one of the characteristic of Medieval historiography.

Most of his works were completed during the reign of Alauddin Khalji or in other words, we can say the reign of Alauddin Khalji was the most productive period of his life. Whose period is known as the Despetic Age[57] of the Early Medieval Indian History. When Alauddin secured the crown by a dramatic "coup-de-main", and advanced to the throne, Khusrau says, "With sword in one hand and gold in other, crowning heads with the latter and severing them with the former".[57] As a result, he could not write any objectionable accounts in his works. Secondly, we can conclude from his early career that he never tried to oppose any circumstance but his principle of life seems to be "to make hay while the sun shines".

Khusrau is well renouned poet and basis of his relationship to the nobles and sultans was his poesy talent. He has tried his best to prove his litrary efficiency in the works. He made the use of contemporary events as the subject of his composition and kept the reality of historical events. With this result most of his works effected with the poetic sensibility and fancy.

The source of information of Amir Khusrau was his own experience or some official records which is not available at present. Any how, he also wrote about his sources of information such as about the sources of *Qiran-us-Sadain.* He writes, "with the table of my heart in my hand, I retired to a corner, my wits confused and my thoughts scattered. I hid myself from my fellow beings-nay, from both men and genii. Soon the stream of ideas arose from my heart and the pen became smoky with the fire of my thoughts".[58] He further says, "whatever the description, I have written in this. I have seen all these. This is not a poem but I have written all the factual description".[59] He also mentions about the, *Miftah-ul-Futuh*" "...... Whatever, has been written in this masnavi, is happened in front of my eyes. I do not increase or decrease in it".[60] About the source of *Dewal Rani-Khizr Khan*, he writes that, "One day the Prince Khizr Khan invites me to his court and requests me to verify the details of his romance with Dewal Devi. After this one slavy gives me a rough draft of the love story. I write this story with a special hard-labour".[61] Later on he continued the narratives to Khizr Khan's death which he had seen with his own eyes.

Similarly, the description of Alauddin Khalji's conquests was based upon his personal knowledge. It seems that while describing the Daccen campaigns of Alauddin Khalji, he himself had gone with Malik Kafur and narrated the eye-seeing events of every day. But it was not possible for him to go with Malik Kafur and his patron Sultan remains in the court;

being a court historian,[62] Khusrau must have based his narratives on authentic official records so that he could mention all the details of the battles without being through the fray himself. Hence we conclude that Amir Khusrau's narration or source of information was his personal knowledge or experience, eyewitness and authentic official records of that time.

Peoples are interested in the past for the variety of reasons. They wish to relive it or draw inspiration from it—they may find that a study of the past helps to give them a better under standing of themselves, of the world in which they live. Some consider the past a useful guide, when making decisions about the future, others find it a source of recreation and intellectual stimulation. In other words peoples learn about the past are as varied as the motives behind their interest in it. Therefore, modern scholars remarks that past was unknown to the Amir Khusrau.

In fact, past was not unknown to him. But past for him was the immediate not, too far. In the *Diwan-wast-ul-Hayat* there are different type of poems. But most of them narrates from the Balban's reign to the death of Prince Muhammad such as Balban's campaigns against the Tughril Khan of Lakhnauti and its success. A few verses are related to the Prince Muhammads conquests of Damrila and Nagarkot, whose rulers refused to pay the *Gaziya*.[63]

The main subject of *Qiran-us-Sadain* was the historical conjunction of Sultan Muizzuddin Qaiqubad and Bughra Khan. But after praises of God and Prophet then followed the description of Delhi, accession of Sultan Quiqubad, the punishment of the Mongols, the triumphal arches, the singing girls, musical instruments, the presents exchanged between Bughra Khan and Qaiqubad, the dishes on the royal table and the different kind of boats used. In this way he enjoy the climaxing the situation and then followed the main subject.

He started to describe the *Dewal Rani Khizr Khan* from the initial conquests of Sultan Alauddin Khalji, conquest of Gujarat, captivity of Dewal Devi (by his commander) to *haram* and followed the main subject, *i.e.*, love story of the prince Khizr Khan and Dewal Devi. He followed the same way of narration in *Tughluq Namah*. He described the victory of Ghiyasuddin Tughluq right from the carelessness of administration by Sultan Mubarak Shah Khalji, conspiracy of Malik Khusrau Khan and the crussification of Alai's princes, etc. So from the above analysis was can conclude that it is not justified to say that Amir Khusrau's works deal with the contemporary incidents or historical events. But after describing the near past or immediate past's incidents systematically and concisely he followed the main subjects.

In the field of subjectivity he was free and despotic writer. Keeping in view he wrote the Historical poems by the order of contemporary sultan such as *Qiran-us-Sadain*, whose main theme is the conjunction of Nasiruddin Bughra Khan and Sultan Muizzuddin Qaiqubad but he starts the fountain of his pen from the description of Delhi, accession of sultan and administration, etc., to the conjunction of son and father (Qaiqubad and Bughra Khan). In historical poem *Miftah-ul-Futuh* he described the four victories of sultan Jalaluddin Khalji with in one year and concluded the historical poem with a prayer for kind and hoping that, "King would recognise the worth of his services which should earn for him an eternal fame".[64] In the same way, he composed the historical poem *Nuh Sipihr* by the request of Sultan Mubarak Shah Khalji for receiving the gold equal to the weight of elephant.[65] But *Sipihr* division clrarly shows that this was full of self satisfaction merit of Amir Khusrau.

Hence, Amir Khusrau composes his verses or prose works by the order of Sultan, on the other hand, the subject-material clears that he was free to choose the subject-material and despotic. Basically, his objects were controlled by the lost of of wealth as well as eternal fame. Perhaps, he was well known to the fact that history cannot be written on each and every events but on a few selected events. In this way he had narrated the selected incidents in his historical poems but did not assert himself as a historian in any work.

He seems to followed the theory of causation.[66] I think Amir Khusrau was one of the first early Medieval Indian Historians, who followed the theory of causation in describing the historical events such as in the *Diwan Wast-ul-Hayat*—a a masnavi related to prince Muhammad conquests of Damrila and Nagarkot.[67] Before describing the punitive campaign of sultan Jalaluddin Khalji against the Malik Chajju of Kara, he described the causes of his campaign in brief.[68] He described the results of the Daccen conquests of Allauddin Khalji which were indirectly providing the causes of conquests.[69] In the historical poem, *Tughluq Namah* he begins his description with the causes of decline of Mubarakshah Khalji or his carelessness towards the administration and different phases of the Ghaji Malik's conquests.[70] In this way Amir Khusrau had described the causes and results of the campaigns and conquests of his patron's. Particularly his description regarding the downfall of the Khalji Dynasty and establishment of Tughluq Sultanate, has its own historical importance.

Amir Khusrau narrated the historical events or facts in the ornate, verbose, penegyric style but did not allow to distort the reality or actuality. Further he adopted the suggestive and instructive[71] method to narrate the facts. By which it seems that the purpose of narration for him is a lesson in future, *e.g.* A decree of Sultan Alauddin Khalji to prince Frid.[72] He eulogises and praises the works of Sultan, Amirs and Maliks. By this method he made to sit the sultan on a high pevelion and narrated their works and conquests. Therefore, it was difficult to narrate the campaigns full of hardships or objectionable to his patron, *e.g.*, the conspiracy of Siddi Maula in reign of Sultan Jalaluddin Khalji, revolts during the reign of Alauddin Khalji or Hardships during the Chittor conquest. Perhaps, by such narrations, he has to face the difficulties or give up his all means of earnings. This also create a hindrance in his writing method.

Although he narrated the historical events very carefully in a ornates, rhetorics, verboses and eulogistics way without distorting the reality or facts such as the tyranny of Alauddin

Khalji[73] and distribution of gold,[74] crusification of Khizr Khan,[75] administrative carelessness of Mubarak Shah Khalji[76] etc. All these examples show that Amir Khusrau narrated the historical facts in the literary language and fully utilised his literary efficiency. This literary efficiency creates a problem to the modern historians. The names of people and places and the continuity of events are not based on his hypothesis.[77] Possibly, none of the chroniclers of our study period, could provide such a description of the political condition right from the Sultan Balban to Ghiyasuddin Tughluq. Even our historian Barani also cited him as his source of information such as Jalaluddin Khalji's behaviour with the rebels.[78] The economic regulations introduced by Sultan Alauddin Khalji are also confirmed by his brief narration.[79] It also seems that perhaps Barani's instructions to the rulers, nobles and soldiers narrated in *Fatawa-i-Jahandari* are the enlargification of the instructions narrated by Amir Khusrau in *Nuh Sipihr*.[80]

Similarly, Isami might have a study of Amir Khusrau's works, *e.g.*, the narration of marriage of Dewal Rani and Khizr Khan.[81] Malik Kafur's conspiracy against Prince Khizr Khan and the desperation of Sultan Alauddin Khalji.[82] Further, he also followed the Amir Khusrau in the description of Ghaji Malik's letters to the different nobles, his soldiers's behaviour to Hindus.[83] Even Ibn-i-Batutta also followed him.[84] Similarly, Abdur Quadir Badauni and Yahya-bin-Ahmad Sirhindi also followed his[85] except a few narrations. In this way it will be cleared that Amir Khusrau narrated the factual information or material which was fully utilized by the contemporary or later chronicler of the study period and asserted themselves a historial.

Amir Khusrau has been successfully narrated the graphic details of wars without any checks while Barani was not so efficient in narrating the wars or campaigns. There are two possible causes first, he had a full knowledge of wars and its tactics.[86] Secondly, he had a personally experience of a soldier. By which he narrated the wars efficiently and even without any checks or hinderences. His wars [descriptions, were providing us the information about the organisation, marches, halts and weapons of the military.[87]

Amir Khusrau does not write anything objectionable to the rulers but he tries to provides the factual position by his ornatic, eulogistic, and verbosic method. In other words, with the help of his writing-method he narrates the impartial description of the period, *e.g.*, he pointed out to the ambitions of Sultan Alauddin Khalji that he desired to conquer the new territorries with the help of Deogir's war-booty. Further when he advanced towards the throne as he says, "with sword in one hand and gold in the other, crowning heads with the latter and severing them with the former".[88] Similarly in *Dewal-Rani-Khizr Khan* he added a suppliment of 319 couplets regarding the crucification of prince Khizr Khan after the death of Sultan Mubarak Shah Khalji.[89] It shows that he described the facts in his own way or method.

The writing method of Barani that—"puts his words in other's mouth", was not his originated method. But Amir Khusrau introduced this method for the fiirst time in his historical poem *Tughluq Namah*. In which he tried to speak out his narrations to the other's months as the two persons are talking and third one is narrating their conversation, *e.g.*, when Khusrau Khan murdered his patron Mubarak Shah Khalji, his associates opposed the nomination of Alai Prince in these words, "when you murder your own master then you will acquire the throne, otherwise you will not be spared by anyone".[90] When Ghaji Malik hears the tyranny of Khusrau Khan, he burns with the fire of revenge but his son Fakhruddin Junna Khan was a courtier and imprisoned by Khusrau Khan. So he could not express his revenge openly, when his son reached Deopalpur and pacified him with these words, "I was waiting for you, now I will try my best to take revenge of my master (Mubarak Shah Khalji)".[91]

After the victory over Khusrau Khan, he rode straightly to the royal palace and called all surviving maliks and amirs to his presence to discuss with them the future of the throne of

Delhi. He told them, "How he a mere soldier of fortune had been taken into service by Jalaluddin, who raised him to a high position. After his death, I remain in a state of confusion as soon as the sun of Alai fortune arises, I joined the services of King. First, I served the Ulagh Khan, the brother of king and enjoys his generousity. When he died then I became the servant of king by the liberity of his blessings, I have seen this place".[92] At last, the nobles pointed out with a humble reverence that—"No prince of Alai family left and that—the crown can be your's. If there will be other able person the God will present this respect to him".[93] In this way Amir Khusrau narrated the conversation of Ghaji Tughluq, maliks and amirs. Possibly, he was the innovator of this writing method that—"put his own words in other's mouth". After his death Barani followed this method on a large scale in his *Tarikh-i-Ferozshahi.*

He narrated impartial and factual material. He never tried to hid the objectives of writing, therefore he mentioned that poem is written to receive the gold or generousity of the ruler, etc. To maintain impartiality and exactness of events he followed the verbose and ornate method, *e.g.*, description of Malik Chajju's revolt,[94] Jhain palace,[95] distribution of gold and jewels by Sultan Alauddin Khalji,[96] difficulties faced by the royal army during the campaign of Tilang and seige of Warangal Fort,[97] Ghaji Malik and his associates army faced a terrible and tough encounter of Khusrau Khan's army at Lahrawat.[98] He recognised the customs of Hindus on the basis of social and religious life while the contemporary or latter chroniclers disliked.

Amir Khusrau narrated the events in a systematically and chronologically order which is varified from the contemporary coins or other archeological monuments, etc., such as conquests of Alauddin.[99] Similarly the decrees, victory-letters were composed in the *Ijaz-i-Khusrau* also increase the information regarding the Sultan's works. So the historical importance of his works increased.

It is well known that Amir Khusrau's works are full of contemporary political material such as the position of Sultan and their works, conquests, position of the nobility, their careers and characters, etc. Keeping in view the position of contemporary rules, he expressed his ideas about the powers and position of Sultan. Particularly he provides the information regarding the theory of state of Alauddin Khalji. He says, "O, King ! God provides you a how much regards, you should follow the "Shara" or Muslim law because it is a pious dead, state also gets respect with religion".[100] It shows that he believes in Divine Theory of State and King is His representative on the earth. He also described the five condition of *Jahandari*.[101] In other words, it can be concluded that the ruler has to establish such administration that provides prosperity and peace to the rich and poor one's.[102] He had a particular views regarding the ruler that, "All the rulers are decoit. They have merits as well demerits—their merits are merits and demerits are the only demerits".[103]

His works also provide us the information regarding the position of nobility and administration such as Prince Muhammad's campaigns against the Damrila and Nagarkot, description about the administration of Sultan Muizzuddin Qaiqubad,[104] the associates of Jalaluddin Khalji and Malik Chajju,[105] character and achievements of Malik Kafur,[106] supporters of Alauddin Khalji,[107] Khusrau Khan[108] and Ghaji Malik,[109] role of nobility in appointing and removing the Sultan.[110]

Like wise, his works also provided the information regarding the administration of contemporary Sultans such as he eulogised the administration of Muizzuddin Quaqubad in *Qiran-us-Sadain* and compared with the *Jamshed's* administration. Similarly he writes that after the accession of Jalaluddin Khalji people were loyal to him.[111] He also narrated in brief the facts of Sultan Alauddin Khalji's administration[112] which are helpful to the verification of late chronicles. He further narrated the carelessness of administration as well as the conspiracy and his tyrannical deeds of Malik Kafur.[113]

Although his Diwans are full of the panegyrics of contemporary nobles. Besides the Sultan he also wrote the masnavians on Hamidu-ddaula, Fakhruddin, Prahlad Tughluq, Muizzulhaq, Alam Alp Khan, Malik Ikhtiyaruddin Sadi, Khan-i-Shahid in *Baqiah Naqiah*". However, his Diwans are full of the rhetorical panegyrics of the contemporary sultan and nobles. Perhaps these nobles would be the prominent figures among the contemporary court. It may be possible the object of writing the suggestions to *amirs*, *maliks* and soldiers[114] as the unstable, changeable attitude of the nobility.

Amir Khusrau's works also provides us the narrations regarding the economic condition of the contemporary society as well as the economic reforms of the sultans which are very important to verify the later chronicles, such as about the economic regulations of the Alauddin Khalji, he writes, "The taxes on the merchants are reduced for the benefit of commoners, with the result they also reduced the prices of articles. All the measures of weight are constructed with iron whose weight written at par. Efficient *Muhtasibs* were appointed to control the black-marketeers, profiteers. If they weighted the less weight, so the same weight became *Tauk* for their necks. When ever there was natural calamity the prices were stabilised by supplying the grains from the royal grainaries.[115] He further narrated that Sultan Alauddin Khalji had been constructed a *Dar-ul-Adl*, distinct features of the market and the variety of clothes.[116] Sultan Alauddin Khalji had an interest in foreign trade. Unfortunately, he did not mention the articles those were exported to Arab, Habbah (Ethopia), Bahran, Barbar, Magrib and Syria.[117]

Narrations of Amir Khusrau also provide us the knowledge of contemporary architectures. This gives corroborative evidence so necessary to the study of history such as the description of the Delhi city,[118] Sultan Qaiqubad's place of Kilo-Kheri,[119] palace of Jhain's Rai,[120] construction and re-construction of the different buildings, Mosques, forts etc., by the Sultan Alauddin Khalji[121] and Mubarak Shah Khalji,[122] desc ription of Multan, Devgiri, Dwara-Samudra, Awadh and

Bengal are also very picturesque. The beautiful description of Tughluqabad fort and palace also find in an ode in the "Diwan-Nihayat-ul-Kamal".[123]

Amir Khusrau also narrated the economic condition of the common people—the main profession of people were agriculture and labour. He further narrated the different professions of the people such as carpenters, blacksmiths, goldsmiths, money-changers or *Sarraf*, oil presser's or *Raughangran*, black-marketeers, hoarders or *Muhtakiran*, singers, dancers, courtesans or *Pakoban*, *Tawaif* and *Ruspiyan*, mimics, acrobats, jugglers, conjurors or *Mushabbid*, *Bazigar*, *Gadan*, *Ghazian*, rope-dancer or *Rasanbazan* gamblers or *Muqamiran*, weavers or *Julaha*, spinner or *Tanindah*, cloth merchant or *Bazzaz*, grain-merchants or *Challa Faroshan*, *Khaiyyat*, tailors, armour-maker or *Zirah-gar*, bow-maker or *Kamangar*, mason, barber or *Hajjam*, cobbers, embroiders, fishermen or *Malugiran*, snake-charmers or *Margiran*, etc.

Amir Khusrau has also narrated about the professional workers condition that some of them were good and lived by their honest and industrious labour while others were definitely bad and dishonest. He did not even spare the learned and mystic sufis for their greedy, hypocrites among them and considered the laity to be a "hundred times better then the priestly class".[124] On other hand, about the low class wage earners he appreciatively writes-that thep pour and sweat of their brow to earn their lawful food, they work with their teeth in the leather to serve mankind. He has very good words to say about the tailors, cobbers and weavers. He also praised the sculptors and masons of Delhi.

He has also narrated the different rates of interest and the condition of money-lenders. He wrote that there were 150 different rates of interest.[125] The rate of interest was one *Jital* per *Tanka* or 20 per cent per year. But there was also a reference of ten per cent per year.[126] Perhaps, it was fixed on the huge amounts. In this way, Amir Khusrau's works provide us valuable source-materials about the economic conditions of the society. People used to earn their livelihood by means of different professions. Although, the main professions of people were the cultivation of land and labour. In short, all these narrations are utmost important for the writing of economic history of the realms.

Amir Khusrau has too given the narrations of contemporary social condition of the society, which prevailed in the society such as diet and drinks, houses, dress, mode of recreation, condition of women, customs and tradition, etc. First, he informs us that there were more than one thousand kinds of cooked, sent in nine tripod trays, from the royal kitchen to the table[127] such as *Nan, Nan-i-Turi* (of Turkish or Mongol variety), "Kak" (a dry biscuit or bread), *Sambosa* (a kind of small pastry of mixed meat of a triagular form) consisting three elements of *Asar,*[128] *Barra-i-Biryan* (Fried or roasted kid), *Mutton chop* (fibs of goat), *Polaw*, fats of the thick tail of *Dumba*[149] variety of birds—*Waji* (guail), *Tihu,*[130] *Durry* (black-patridge), *Charz,*[131] *Halwa, Cakes of Sabuni,*[132] *Fuqqa*[133], *Sherbat*, etc.

Ijaz-i-Khusrawi contains the reference of to many articles of food such as *Kabab, Zaliba-i-Nabat*[134], *Sirka, Jughrat*[135], *Girda-i-Paneer, Paludah,*[136] *Murabba,*[137] *Sikbat* or *Sikbati*[138] *Khushka,*[139] *Shakkar Paich,*[140] *Ruqaq,*[141] *Tutmaj, Lauzina,*[143] *Sarabi-i-Asir, Sharb-i-Naishkar,*[142] *Sikanjabin,*[144] *Ghulaha khar,*[145] *Qaisunqur, Bughra*[146] and *Shulla*[147]. In the long discource of volume-II of *Ijaz-i Khusrawi* in which we find the forty two merits mentioned as against the forty three demerits of "Betel and Betel Chewing".

Amir Khusrau gives us a peep into the "Dark Corners" of people,[148] thatched houses of the poor one's.[149] On other hand he takes into the high roofed, two storied houses of the rich people and upper class which had vaulted halls,[150] pool of water,[151] bathroom,[152] library,[153] courtyard,[154] threshold,[155] portico,[156] with lofty pillars, painted walls and high doorways.[157]

He has told us about the clothes attire and adore. They were of the various stuffs or tissue, silken, cotton, woollen, linen, embroidered, painted and the gold and silver work such as—*Khaz*, *Deba*, *Harir*, *Zarbaft*, *Zardozi*, *Makhmal*, *Atlas*, *Daq*, *Katan*, *Kirpas*, *Parneen*, *Aksun*, etc. He is very lavis in praise of the cloths of Devgiri, Bihar and Awadh especially the first.[158] Similarly the types and modes of dress have also been referred to such as *Daster-Bandan*, *Mutammiamah* and *Kulahdaran*[159] The other cloths were *Pairahan*, *Qaba*,[160] *Aba*,[161] *Jubba*,[162] *Rida*[163] *Saravil*[164], *Lungi*, *Barani*,[165] *Shalwar*, *Dotai*. The garments of women were "Naqab", *Magna*, *Durrah'a*, *Paecha*, *Chadar*, *Qasb*, *Izar or Kishtak*, *Pairahan*, *Reshaha-i-Damani*, *Gulband*, Chirinbaf and also referred to the clothes of Sufis and Darveshes.[166]

Amir Khusrau has also told us about the cosmetics and toilets. It was a popular craze to look young even though youth had receded beyond recall. Women used to beautify themselves with the antimony and *Kazzal* for eyes,[167] *Khizab*[168] for hairs, powder for face and *Henna*[169] or myrtle for hands, feet and fingers tips. He also satired at the middle aged women who used to beautify herself,[170] and suggested to women the natural and some modes of beautification.[171] He was extremely orthodox and conservative in his attitude towards the fair sex.

He has also referred to some of the typical customs and traditions of Hindu such as *Parda-Pratha* (curtain-system) and its importance,[172] "a hindu wife immolated herself on the pyre of her husband",[173] *i.e.*, *Sati-Piath*, *Jauhar Pratha*,[174] drinking of water, out of hands of their palms,[175] use of vermillion on their forehead by Hindus.[176] He also referred to the *Jalwe*[177] tradition (meeting of the bride and bridegroom) is not that to look like a bedecked idol or fairy before the husband, but to be bestiful, modest and fearful and to be known and seen from behind the curtain mounted with fringed of the veil".

Amir Khusrau has also referred to some means of amusement prevailing in the society such as hunting, chess,[178]

Pollow,[179] dances,[180] different music instruments, rope-dancers, acorbats conjurors, masqueraders, enchanters,[181] wrestling, snake-charmer,[182] etc. He also referred to the celebration of some festivals or important occassions such as—*Nauroj*,[183] *Shabb-i-Rat*,[184] birth day,[185] victory-cerbration, coronation etc.

Amir Khusrau's observation of the ways of the sots and drunkards *Rabis* (usurers), *Rashis* (bribers), *Zanis* (adulters) and also *Muthakiran* (horders and profiteers) show that, such vices were prevalent in his time. He narrated that a drunkard *Mu-ezzin* who entered the magnificent mosque of a Qazi Imran in a state of intoxication and the smell of liquor coming out of his mouth defiled the pillars and refters of mosque[186], Ulemas poured liquor in the same bosom in which the Quran was treasured.[187] In the *Khazain-ul-Fatuh* we noticed that, "account of wine bibing the author was himself a teetolaller give an indirect hint to the Alauddin's prohibition of the drinking and sale of wine, how the roots of all inequities, lust and adultery were cut off...prostitutes get married, he uprooted the *Ibahati*.[188]

Amir Khusrau also deals with a lot of Indian themes and elements which shows his patrotic sentiments had grown wider and deeper so it did not remain confined to Delhi only but he had been grasping extraordinary amount of love for every thing which was Indian also such as praise of Delhi,[189] enlogreson of Sanskrit language eulogised,[190] admiration of Jhain fortress,[191] Admiration for Indian flowers and beauties,[192] Indian Marriage ceremonies,[193] worship of fire,[194] the greatness of India,[195] affectionate feelings for Hindu learning and religion,[196] Indian languages,[197] Indian animals and birds,[198] Indian Magicians,[199] betel leaf.[200] Likewise, the features of Amir Khusrau's writing of India is that he does not suffer from the customary prejudice of Medieval chroniclers.

The writings of Amir Khusrau are of the immense value to us historically as well. Living in the capital of Delhi Sultanate had a close contact with the nobles, Princes and Sultans. He witnessed historic events and was himself present in some of the military campaigns. He narrated factual material in his works which was fully utilised by the others historians such as Barani, Isami, Ibn-i-Batutta, Ferishta, Badauni, and asserted themselves as a historian but Amir Khusrau never asserted himself as a historian.

He has referred the detailed accounts of expeditions, campaigns and wars but our historian Barani failed to do so. Because Amir Khusrau was himself a soldier and had a full knowledge of the war tactics. He narrated a impertial description of events in ornate, verbose, rhetoric, panygric and suggestive method, by which he did not allow the distortion or mis-representation of the factor actuality. He was the innovator of new writing method that, "to put his own words in others mouth" which was fully used by Barani in his book, *Tarikh-i-Ferozshahi* on the large scale.

Modern historians blaims that, Amir Khusrau write in verbostic, rhetoric, eulogistic and ornatice style and hesitated to recognise him as a historian. He used to ornates just to describe a minor incident. He did not distort the historical facts by using ornatic language such as title of "Alaxander II", "Shadow of God", "Caliphate of the Era", description of the marriage of Dewal Rani and Khizr Khan,[201] implementation of the decree of crucification of princes,[202] etc.

Although, he used the verbostic, ornatic, eulogistic language for the narrations of events. We should not blame him before keeping in view his position and contemporary circumstances. First, he wrote the works and dedicated to the Sultans. Second, he was a courtier. Third, he wrote the maximum books during the despotic rule of Alauddin Khalji. Fourth, he was first a poet then a narrator. Therefore, he fully utilised his literary efficiency in describing the actuality and facts. He himself wrote that truth has a separate delight. Therefore, he followed the contemporary feature of writing that eulogises and panygrics of the works of the nobles and Sultans which was not only the fault of our writer but was a tone of the period.

Amir Khusrau's writing about India does not suffer from

the customary prejudices of Muslim chroniclers of that time such as Barani, Isami, etc. Although he does not agree with the main tenets of Hindu religion and customs but he shows a deep sense of appreciation of this ancient culture such as—In *Dewal Rani Khizr Khan* has described. A Hindu devotes worshiping fire and explained that the fire enlightened in his heart the hope of union and in persishing into it, he earned perennial life, he advices his readers to have respect for his sublime emotion and high sense of devotion.[203] In *Nuh Sipihr* has described the some aspects of Hinduism such as—"They did not follow his religion but most of their beliefs were similar to his religious ideal. They also had conviction that God is One. He is Eternal. He is the Inventor. He is the Creater. He is the giver of livelihood. He is Omnipotent.[204]

Further, he did not like to compare Hinduism with Islam but by making comparision with all other religions of world, he considered it better than all of them, for, which he offered the following reasons : "Dualists believed that there were two Gods but Hindus believed in oneness of God. The Christians think that Christ was the son of God but Hindus did not accept this view... The fire worshipers through light and darkness as two goods but the Hindus had no such conception. They worship stones (Idols), animals and tress but the spirit of their sincerity in worshipping them is worth of being respected. They believed that all these things have been created by one Creator. They do not disobey this Creator. They worship them only because their ancestors have been worshipping them."[205] In this way it can be concluded that Amir Khusrau was not too prejudicious like the Barani and Isami. He had not soft corner for Mongols whom he considered enemies either of his motherland or of the crown. He always used harsh words and phrases for them.[206] But once they became loyal to the crown and displayed a sense of religious political and social toleration.

Amir Khusrau stated his work with panygirics of God, his saint which was the main feature of medieval historical writings because all the educational institution were under the influence of religious institutions. All the chroniclers of that period tried to hid the weaknesses of their patron and blamed a mystic power for their demerits as well as defeates. Therefore, the students of such institutions and period naturally be influenced. He was a true follower of Islam but had some patience towards the non-muslims.

Amir Khusrau has also referred to geographical description but the name of these places are not traced by the modern historians, so they considered it as his fault. It is right that Amir Khusrau described the graphic description of Daccen campaigns of Malik Kafur but modern historian failed to trace the way of the campaigns as narrated by him. So they are doubtful about his geographical description. But it is not justified to compare the names of 13th or 14th century to those of the modern times. The change in name is natural, we should not blame him for the changing or untraceability.

Some scholars say that Amir Khusrau had tried to hide the facts which were well known to him. No doubt, they are quite right to some extent. But before blaming him, we should keep in view his conditions or contemporary cirumstances such as the in *Miftah-ul Futuh* he narrated the only victories of Sultan but did not refer to the conspiracy of Siddi Maula, in *Khazain-ul-Futuh* he did not refer to the full description of Chittor conquest, attack of Qatlug Khawaja[207] and three revolts.

We should keep in view of his objects of writings that he wrote *Miftah-ul-Futuh* to receive the generosity of Sultan, if he describe the attack of Mongols and conspiracy of Siddi Moula. Possibly, he would not successful in his object to receive the generosity of Sultan because Sultan was successful in the beginning but was forced to sign a treaty with Mongols, similarly in the conspiracy of Siddi Maula he has to face the opposition of the *Ulemas*. Therefore, he did not refer to the conspiracy of Siddi Maula and it was also against their nature. If he describe the conspiracy possibly it could not be popular in the Muslim world and sultan would be annoyed.

Similarly, Khusrau designated the Sultan Alauddin Khalji as "Alaxander-II" and described his conquests in *Khazain-ul-Futuh*.

If he described the attack of Qatlug Khawaja, he has to face the difficulty in proving his patron Alauddin as a "Alaxander-II". Therefore, he did not narrate the attack of Qatlugh Khawaja and internal revolts. Possibly he had also a fear of Sultan in this way, he did not narrate the difficulties faced by the Sultan Alauddin Khalji during the conquest of Chittor.

In this way after a critical analysis of the Khusrau's life and works, we are able to conclude that he has narrated the historical events from the reign of Sultan Balban to the death of Ghiyasuddin Tughluq and accession of Muhammad bin-Tughluq. He had narrated the political, social, economic and relegious condition of the realm or variety people, *i.e.*, Sultan, nobility and commoners in ornate, rhetoric, panygric and verbose language. There is not lack of candour and impartiality. There may be some omissions but not distortions or misrepresentation of the facts and actuality.

He was the innovator of Barani's writing method, "To put his words in the other's mouth". A chronology of Alauddin conquests, Daccen campaigns and Mongol incursion during Alauddin Khalji's reign can be sketched out on the basis of Amir Khusrau's narrations. Modern historian agree with the historical importance of *Khazain-ul-Futuh* as it is the only contemporary chronicle of Alauddin Khalji's reign and narrates facts honestly. Each portion of the *Qiran-us-Sadian* has been represented from objective and subjective point of view. Amir Khusrau was the first greatest Indian patriot because no single person or group has enumarated so many points of merits and of excellence of India, seperately or collectively and proved India superior to the whole world.

Amir Khusrau was first a poet and literary man than a narrator of historical facts or events. In fact, his narration of facts or moral obligation, "to tell the truth and nothing but only the truth", that makes him more acceptable to the historians of that age such as Barani, Isami, Batuttah, Ferishta, Badauni, etc. even to the modern historian also. Therefore, we should not hesitate to honour him for his labour that he was the first National-Poet-Historian of early Medieval Indian History for which he did not assert in his works.

REFERENCES

1. Amir Khusrau belonged to a noble family "Lachin", see—M.W. Mirza, *The Life and Works of Amir Khusrau*, Delhi, 1974, pp. 6-13.
2. For detail see—*Ibid.*, pp. 15-16.
3. *Ibid* , *Dibacha of Tuhfat-us-Sigar*, as cited on p. 20.
4. *Ibid.*, p. 21.
5. Dr. Dension Ross, *Catalogue of the Bankipur Library*, 1908, p. 178.
6. A. Khusrau was born in 651 A.H. and it was according to his own version, he was eight years old at the time of his father's death which give us the year 659 A.H./1261 A.D.
7. It is said that the great saint Hazarat Nizamuddin Auliya, 'Mahboob-i-Ilahi' used to staying at the Imad-ul-Mulk's residence.
8. Khusrau's Musical contribution—see—S. Sarmadee, "Musical Genius of Amir Khusrau", pub. in *Memorial Volume—Amir Khusrau*, New Delhi, 1975, pp, 33-61.
9. Nawab Haj Mohammad Ishak Khan, *Prolegomena to An Edition of the Collected Works of Amir Khusrau*, Delhi, 1917, p. 4.
10. Amir Khusrau as a great Indian Patriot—see—S.A. Sandilvi, "A Great Indian Patriot", pub. in *Memorial Volume—Amir Khusrau, op. cit.*, pp. 21-23 : A. Khusrau, *Nuh Sipihr*, Islamic Research Association, 1950, pp. 149-61, 166-72, 178-81, 193.
11. Gyasuddin Balban, Mizzuddin Qaiqubad, Jalaluddin Khalji, Alauddin Khalji, Qutabuddin Mubarak Shah Khalji, Ghiyasuddin Tughluq and accession of Muhammad-bin-Tughluq.

12. He saw the Mangol hordes marching into the country, personally experienced their torture in the captivity, fought against Tughril Khan at Lakhauti during the reign of Balban, eye-witness to the historic meetings of Bughra Khan and Sultan Qaiqubad, saw the estabishment of Khalji dynasty, accompanied Jalaluddin Khalji's campaign to Kara and Jhain, followed Alauddin Khalji's campaign to Chittor, according to Badauni he had gone came to the Far-South with Malik Kafur. He witnessed the tragic end of Alauddin, his family beings ruthlessly messacred by Malik Kafur and the tragic end of Qutabuddin Mubarak Shah Khalji by Malik Khusrau Khan, etc.

13. Barani, *Tarikh-i-Ferozshahi*, Calcutta, 1860-62, p. 113.

14. For detail of trival incident—see—M.W. Mirza, *op. cit.*, p. 39-40.

15. Amir Khusrau joined his court in 673 A.H./1274 A.D.

16. For detail account see— *Ibid.*, pp. 38-44.

17. Barani, *op. cit.*, p. 69.

18. *Ibid.*, p. 109 : For detail of campaign and the death of Muhammad—A. Khusrau, *Diwan-Wastul-Hapat*, Aligarh, n.d., p. 161-69.

19. *Ibid.*, p. 110 : A.A.A Rizvi, *Adi Turk Kalin Bharat*, Aligarh, 1956, p. 285.

20. A. Khusrau, *Qiran-us-Sadain*, Aligarh, 1918, pp. 221-22.

21. *Ibid.*, p. 231.

22. Qaiqubad's Epiqurean—see—Barani, *op. cit.*, pp. 128-31.

23. Writing of this historical poem might have been started in May, 1289 A.D.

24. A. Khusrau, *Ibid.*, pp. 234-35.

25. Keeper of the royal copy of the Qur'an—see—Barani, *op. cit.*, p. 198.

26. *Ibid.*, p. 197.
27. *Ibid.*, p. 200.
28. A. Khusrau, *Miftah-ul-Futuh*, Aligarh, 1954, p. 40.
29. Patron of Khaqani, was the son of Minuchihr Shirwan Shah.
30. M.W. Mirza, *op. cit.*, p. 87.
31. K.A. Nizami, ed., *Politics and Society During the Early Medieval Period*, New Delhi, 1974, Vol. I, p. 304.
32. Barani, *op. cit.*, p. 366. But Twelve hundred tankas would be more accurate. This was the Khusrau's annual salary as a government officer.
33. For detail see—A. Khusrau, *Nihayat-ul-Kamal*, (B.M. Ms., 125, 807) f. 469b, as cited by M.W. Mirza, *op. cit.*, p. 131, f.n. 2.
34. Ferishta, *Tarikh-i-Ferishta*, Newal Kishore Press, Lucknow, Vol. I, p. 132.
35. Means that the beloved lies on the couch with her block tresses scattered on her face. O Khusrau ! Return to your home for night has fallen all over the world-Brij Rattan Dass, *Khusrau Ki Hindi Kavita*, Kashi, 2010 V.S., p. 3.
36. Chapterisation, subjectivity, divisions and sub-divisions of the books, dots, vowel, some typical word or pharases of special interest, etc.—see—M.W. Mirza, *op. cit.*, p. 140, ascited in fn. I., p. 141.
37. See Barani, writes that Amir Khusrau written a whole library in poetry and prose, *op. cit.*, p. 359.
38. Jami, *Mafahat-ul-Uns*, ed. by Nassau less, Calcutta, 1859, p. 710.
39. Spenger's, *Catalogue of the Oudh King's Library*, MSS. Vol. I, pp. 465 on wards.
40. Nawab Haj Mohammad Ishaq Khan, *op. cit.*, p. 27.
41. *Ibid.*, p. 28.

42. M.W. Mirza, *op. cit.*, p. 149.
43. For [detail—see—*Ibid.*, pp. 152-73 ; L.S. Chandel, *Khalji Kalin Itihaskar-Ke Rup Main Amir Khusrau*, H.P.U. Simla MS. 1977, pp. 38-39.
44. See-*Ibid.*, pp. 174-190, *Ibid.*, pp. 40-46.
45. *Ibid.*, pp. 190-203.
46. *Ibid.*, pp. 203-15.
47. *Ibid.*, pp. 216-27, L.S. Chandel, *op. cit.*, p. 46-49.
48. *Ibid.*, pp. 227-32, Brij Rattan Dass, *op. cit.*, pp. 19-52.
49. Barani, *op. cit.*, pp. 10-11.
50. *Ibid.*, p. 11.
51. *Ibid.*, pp. 12-13.
52. *Qiran-us-Sadian*, pp. 231-35.
53. *Ibid.*, pp. 236-56.
54. A. Khusrau, *Tughluq Namah*, Hydrabad, 1933, p. 14.
55. *e.g.*, Barani, Isami, Ferishta, Badauni, etc.
56. R.P. Tripathi, *Some Aspects of Muslim Administration*, Allahabad, 1956, pp. 42-54.
57. As cited by M.W. Mirza, *op. cit.*, p. 88, fn. 2, I.O. MS. 1187, fol. 817b seq. a long and fine historical poem describing the Alauddin's exploits.
58. *Qiran-us-Sadain*, p. 233.
59. *Ibid.*, p. 256.
60. *Miftah-ul-Futuh*, p. 39.
61. A. Khusrau, *Dewal Rani Khizr Khan*, Aligarh, 1917, pp. 38-46.
62. M.W. Mirza, *op. cit.*, p. 105.
63. *Dewan-Wast-ul Hayat*, verses-86-145. He writes about the Muhammad's conquest against Mongols, their features, murder of Prince Muhammad, his (Khusrau) captivity, etc.

64. *Miftah-ul-Futuh*, p. 40.

65. M.W. Mirza, *op. cit.*, p. 125.

66. According to Prof. Gustavson, "Cause is a convenient figure of speech for any one of a number of factors which helps to explain why a historical event happened". Carl. G. Gustavson, *A Preface to History*, New York, 1955, p. 55, for causation see—Louis Gottsehalk, *Understanding History—A Premier of Historical Method*, New York, 1956, p. 227.

67. Khusrau described that price led a punitive expedition against the King of Damila and Nagarkot, Kangra, who were refused to pay, "Jaziya" and made them submissive. See—*Wast-ul-Hayat*, verses-86-145.

68. *Miftah-ul-Futuh*, pp. 8-22.

69. For example—conquest of Deogir, Arangal, Dawarsamudr, Mabar-see-A. Khusrau, "*Khazain-ul-Futuh*, Aligarh, 1924, pp. 70-182. He narrated the causes as well as the results of the conquests. Even we can guess from the causes that what may be the causes of conquests ?

70. Detail of causes-see-*Tughluq Namah*, pp. 17-21, for the Ghaji Malik causes of conquests and result—see—62, causes see—pp. 37-86, for results, pp. 131-51.

71. *Nuh-sipihr*, pp. 228-42, 251-54, 256-57.

72. For detail see—A. Khusrau, *Ijar-i-Khusrawi*, Lucknow, Vol. IV, pp. 119 Seq.

73. M.W. Mirza, *op. cit.*, p. 89.

74. *Khazain-ul-Futuh*, p. 11.

75. *Dewal Rani Khizr Khan*, pp. 274-79.

76. *Tughluq Namah*, pp. 17-19.

77. The views of modern historian about the "Dewal Rani Khizr Khan", is that heroin "Dewal Rani" is a hypotheses of poet not a reality.

78. Barani, *op. cit.*, p. 183.

79. *Ibid.*, pp. 302-19, information verified from the Khusrau's narration in the *Khazain-ul-Futuh*, pp. 15-24.

80. For comparison see—Barani, "Fataw-I-Jahandari", (I.D. Ms. No. 2563) ff. 2*a*-8*a*, 45*a* 58*a*, 64*a*-73*a*, 100*a*-101*a*, 104*a*-105*a* ; *Nuh Sipihr*, pp. 228-57.

81. For detail see—*Dewal Rani Khizr Khan*, pp. 291-323 ; Isami, *Futuh-us-Salatin*, (Madras, 1948), pp. 314-24.

82. For detail see—*Ibid.*, pp. 237-52 ; *Ibid.*, pp. 340-42.

83. For detail see—*Tughluq Namah*, pp. 128-32, *Ibid.*, pp. 379-80.

84. For *e.g.*, see—attach of Khusrau Khan's Military, *Ibid.*, p. 124 ; Ibn-i-Batutta, *Kitab-ul-Rehla*, (Paris, 1949), pp. 48, 49 ; punishment of Khusrau Khan, *Ibid.*, p. 20 ; *Ibid.*, p. 199.

85. Badauni, *Muntakhab-ul-Tawarikh*, (Calcutta, 1868), pt. 1, p. 217 ; A.M. Hussain, *Tughlaq Dynasty*, (Calcutta, 1963), p. 41.

86. Dr. Jagdish Narayan Sarkar, head of the history department in Jadavpur University wrote a paper on the art of war in Medieval Indian on the basis of material available in *Khazain-ul-Futuh*, *Qiran-us-Sadain*, *Diwan Ghurratul Kamal*, *Miftah-ul-Futuh*, *Ashiqia*, *Nuh sipihr*, *Tughluq Namah* and *Ija-i-Khusrawi*—see—*Indo-Iranica*—Amir Khusrau, Sept.-Dec. 1971, pp. 6-36.

87. For example in 683 A.H. he had the fought war against Mongols with his patron Prince Muhammad ; he also accompanied prince Bugra Khan when he proceed to against the Tughril Khan of Lakhnauti, Sultan Jalaluddin Khalji against his former patron Malik Chajju of Kara, in 1303 A.D. he accompanied also Sultan Allauddin Khalji to Chittor conquest.

88. *Miftah-ul-Futuh*, he writes that :

"Va yak dast Ahn, Vayak dasti zar,
Ajin tajdad va ajan burd sur".

Elliot and Dowson, *History of India as told by its own Historians*, Vol. III, p. 392.

89. For detail see—*Dewal Rani Khizr Khan*, pp. 276-87.
90. Khusrau writes, "Thirty thousand horsemen defeated the ten soldiers". See—*Tughluq Namah*, p. 21.
91. *Ibid.*, p. 45.
92. *Ibid.*, pp. 136-38.
93. *Ibid.*, 138-40.
94. *Miftah-ul-Futuh*, p. 8.
95. *Ibid.*, pp. 31-38.
96. *Khazain-ul-Futuh*, p. 11.
97. *Nuh Sipihr*, pp. 93-94.
98. *Tughluq Namah*, p. 124.
99. For example—19, Rabi-ul-Aakhir, 695 A.H./25 February, 1296 A.D., marched to Deogir ; on 28 Rajab, 695 A.H./1 June, 1296 A.D. reached at Kara Manikpur with the war-booty ; Wednesday, 16, Ramazzan, 695 A.H./18 July, 1296 A.D. occupied throne at Kara ; Monday 22, Zilhijja, 695 A.H./21 October, 1296 A.D. he occupied throne at Delhi etc.—in the same way other compaigns are described systematically and chronologically.
100. *Nuh Sipihr*, p. 228.
101. Means Administration or state system.
102. *Ibid.*, pp. 228-257.
103. Hardev, *Chehal Rozah*, (ed. by Kh. Hasar Nizami, Delhi in Urdu), pp. 29-30.
104. *Qiran-us-Sadain*, p. 35.
105. *Miftah-ul-Futuh*, p. 14.
106. *Dewal Rani Khizr Khan*, pp. 236-52.

107. *Izaz-i-Khusrawi*, Vol. IV, pp. 104-19.

108. *Tughluq Namah*, pp. 48-119.

109. *Ibid.*, pp. 1?8-44 ; *Dawal Rani Khizr Khan*, pp. 262-64 ; *Khazain-ul-Futuh*, p. 11.

110. *Qiran-us-Sadain*, p. 35.

111. *Miftah-ul-Futuh*, pp. 7, 8.

112. *Khazain-ul-Futuh*, pp. 15-24.

113. *Dewal Rani Khizr Khan*, pp. 233-64.

114. *Nuh Sipihr*, pp. 251-57.

115. *Khazain-ul-Futuh*, pp. 17, 22.

116. Varieties of clothes from "Kirpas to Harir" which cover the nakedness of body from "Bihari" to "Gul-i-Baqli" which are used both for summer and winter, from shirt or under garments of "Galim" (blanket of goats hair) which differ greatly in their hair ; from "Jaz' to "Khaz" which are similarly engraved or painted from Devgiri to Mahadeo Nagari—*Ibid.*, pp. 23-24.

117. *Ijaz-i-Khusrawi*, Vol. II, p. 319.

118. *Qiran-us-Sadain*, p. 28-34.

119. *Ibid.*, pp. 54-57.

120. *Miftah-ul-Futuh*, pp. 31-32.

121. *Khazain-ul-Futuh*, pp. 25-34.

122. *Nuh-Sipihr*, pp. 77-78.

123. A.A.A. Hanfee, "The historian in Khusrau", published in "Memorial volume—*Amir Khusrau*, p. 178.

124. For detail see—Amir Khusrau, *Matla-ul-Anwar*, (Lucknow, 1884), Ch. VI, he writes that :

> "Hast Base Sufi-i-Pashinina posh-kas na
> rasad bang-i-Muezz, in bagosh......In hamma
> Shai Rhan-i-Khaza in parast-Barhamanand but-i-e—'
> Zarrin ba dart".

125. A. Khusrau, *Kulliyat-i-Khusrawi*, pp. 312.
126. K.M. Ashraf, *op. cit.*, p. 128.
127. For detail see—*Qiran-us-Sadain*, pp. 159-93.
128. "Asar"—Arad, Sorid, Raughan.
129. A kind or type of sheep is more delicious than "Abu-Barra" (fawn).
130. A bird smaller than a patridge.
131. Bustard, a bird of game whose flesh is tender and delicate.
132. A mixture of almoud, honey, sesame oil.
133. A kind of drink made of water and barley and of dried grapes, something like beer.
134. *Ijazi-i-Khusrawi*, Vol. IV, p. 325.
135. *Ibid.*, Vol. IV, p. 51.
136. *Ibid.*, Vol. II, pp. 177, 517.
137. *Ibid.*, Vol. I, p. 169.
138. *Ibid.*, Vol. I, p. 612.
139. *Ibid.*, Vol. I, p. 23.
140. *Ibid.*, Vol. I, p. 196.
141. *Ibid.*, Vol. IV, p. 325.
142. *Ibid.*, Vol. IV, p. 15.
143. *Ibid.*, Vol. IV, p. 53.
144. *Ibid.*, Vol. I, p. 23.
145. *Ibid.*, Vol. I, p. 60.
146. A kind of dish invented by Bughra Khan.
147. *Matla-ul-Anwar*, Ch. II.
148. *Ijaz-i-Khusrawi*, Vol. IV, p. 114.
149. *Ibid.*, Vol. II, p. 18.
150. *Suffa-i-Taq*".

151. *Hauz Khana.*
152. *Ab-Khanna.*
153. *Kitab-Khanna.*
154. *Sahan.*
155. *Dahliz.*
156. *Rawaq.*
157. For detail see—*Ibid.*, Vol. V, pp. 57-61 ; 87-89.
158. *Khazain-ul-Futuh*, p. 24.
159. Large turbans worn by Ulemas and religious group on the head, over a close fitted skull cap called 'Kullah", consequently they were called by these names.
160. Sleeved coat open in front, cloak.
161. A kind of coat or cloak.
162. A species of upper Coat.
163. Mantle.
164. A trouser like peejama.
165. A cloth for keeping off rains.
166. See for detail—*Ijaz-i-Khusrawi*, Vol. I, pp. 1-26.
167. *Matla-ul-Anwar*, p. 186.
168. "Khizab" as a coloured substance used for blackening hair, *Ibid.* p. 173.
169. *Ibid.*, p. 222.
170. For detail see—*Ibid.*, pp. 186-94.
171. *Ibid.*, p. 223.
172. *Ibid.*, p. 159 ; *Ijaz-i-Khusrawi*, Vol. III, p. 317.
173. He writes that, "women burnt herself out of love for her husband"—see—*Nuh Sipihr*, pp. 194-95.
174. *Khazian-ul-Futuh*, pp. 54-59, 88.

175. A Khusrau, *Aina-i-Sikandari*, (Aligarh, 1917-18), p. 32.
176. *Ibid.*, pp. 53-54.
177. *e.g.*, *Dewal Rani Khizr Khan*, pp. 167-68.
178. *Nuh Sipihr*, pp. 169-70.
179. *Kulliyat-i-Khusrawi*, p. 223.
180. *Dewal Rani Khizr Khan*, p. 158.
181. *Ibid.*, pp. 154-57.
182. *Ijaz-i-Khusrawi*, Vol. IV, p. 270.
183. *Qiran-us-Sadain*, pp. 67-77.
184. *Ijaz-i-Khusrawi*, Vol. IV, p. 324.
185. Sixth Sipihr of the *Nuh Sipihr*.
186. *Ibid.*, Vol. IV, p. 175.
187. *Matla-ul-Anwar*, Ch. II, p. 58, also see—*Khazain-ul-Futuh*, pp. 18-21.
188. See—*Khazain-ul-Futuh*, pp. 18-21.
189. *Qiran-us-Sadain*, pp. 28-29 ; *Nuh Sipihr*, pp. 143-47.
190. *Dewal Rani Khizr Khan*, pp. 41-43.
191. *Miftah-ul-Futuh*, pp. 31-32.
192. *Dewal Rani Khizr Khan*, pp. 126-33.
193. *Ibid.*, pp. 154-69.
194. *Ibid.*, pp. 195-96.
195. *Nuh Sipihr*, pp. 150-61, 166-72.
196. *Ibid.*, pp. 160-66.
197. *Ibid.*, pp. 178-81.
198. *Ibid.*, pp. 181-91.
199. *Ibid.*, pp. 191-95.
200. *Qiran-us-Sadain*, pp. 94, 185-86.
201. *Dewal Rani Khizr Khan*, pp. 162-63.

202. *Ibid.*, p. 275.

203. *Ibid.*, pp. 195-96.

204. *Nuh Sipihr*, p. 164.

205. *Ibid.*, pp. 164-66.

206. *Diwan-Wast-ul-Hayat*, pp. 106, 107, 161, etc.

207. He did not narrate the Qatlug Khawaja's attack on Alla-uddin's Sultanate in "Khazain-ul-Futuh" but he narrate this event in *Dewal Rani Khizr Khan*, p. 61.

5

References to Kangra and Sirmur in the Early Medieval Persian Sources

The political history of Himachal Hill States suffers from a serious drawback for the want of an adequate details concerning its history during the early phase of the Turkish expansion in India. The reasons are not too far too seek. The Turkish Sultans were assentially an urban settlers and their activities were confined mostly in plains, fighting against the rebellious chiefs or leading punitive expeditions. Himachal Pradesh as it stands today, had not attained a geographical identity like other states as Punjab, Gujarat, Bengal, Bihar, etc.

Again the persian chroniclers were interested only in vivid description of the Sultan—their court and mobility. They narrated only those events which glorified Islam and where in the Sultan or his commanders attained victories against the infidels.

However, a careful study of the contemporary persian chronicls may reveal some clear references to the punitive expeditions against some of the important states of Himachal Pradesh notably those of Sirmur,[1] Nagarkot.[2] Both these places find frequent references in the persian sources since the begining of the Turkish rule in India. An attempt has been made in the present *papers* to review the activities of the Turkish rulers towards these two leading Hill State of Modern Himachal Pradesh.

Sirmur

The first persian chronicler which contains reference about the Sirmur is Minhajuddin Siraj who completed the *Tabaqat-i-Nasiri* in A.H. 658/1260 A.D. He writes that rebel Malik Nizamulmulk Junaidi[3] lost the faith of his associate as a result of tactful handing of Sultan Raziya and consequently fled towards the Sirmur Hills.[4] There is a similar reference to the flight of Jalaluddin Masul towards the Sirmur Hills during the reign of Sultan Nasiruddin Mahmud.[5]

During the reign of the same Sultan Qatlugh Khan[6] defeated in the battle and seeks shelter with the chief of Santurgarh in Sirmur Hill.[7] Our chronicler writes that—Ulugh Khan-i-Muazzam destroyed these hill territories and reached in the foot hills of Sirmur. Neither any Sultan established his suzerainty nor any army of Islam has so far reached in these region. The place was plundered and destroyed. It is reported that the casualty of Hindus was so great that it was beyond description.[8]

Qatlugh Khan once again emerged from this retreat and occupied Awadh and even sought to capture Kara and Manikpur. However, Arslan Khan who then hold this province succeeded in expelling him and Qatlugh Khan once again was obliged to flee and seek shetler with the chief of Santurgarh in Simur Hills.[9] Minhaj writes that Rana Ranpal helped all those people who sought shetler with him and gave them all assistance.

In A.H. 655/1257 A.D. Balban marched towards Santur with the Delhi Army to attack this area. After crossing the Hill region, he reached the Sirmur territory. Rana Ranpal fled away and his territory was plundered as far his capital and city. Balban succeeded in conquering this territory where no one had reached earlier.[10] However, Balban failed to trace

Qatlugh Khan who once again created a problem for Delhi in A.H. 655/1257 A.D.

During the Khalji Sultanate, we find only a single reference regarding the Sirmur. According to Yahya-bin-Ahmed Sirhindi.[11] The Mogols under the leadership of Muhammod Tartaq and Alibeg marched towards Delhi. One contingent of the army was despatched towards Vivah (Bias) river through Sirmur Hills.[12]

During the Tughluq Sultanate Yahya writes that other the pre-occupation Firozshah marched towards Sirmur Hills for excurssion and sports.[13] The Zamindars of the region submitted to him and subsequently the sultan returned to Delhi after spending four months in this region.[14] It is further reported that Ferozshah Tughluq levied tribute from the Rai of Sirmur and Rais of Hills.[15]

In January 1388 A.D., Prince Muhammad consolidating his position. Sultan Ferozshah led a hunting expendition towards Sirmur Hillts. Where he hunted Wolfs and Gojans for two months.[16] But when Ferozshah had decided to take field against his son Prince Muhammad, the soldiers deserted the prince on seeing their old master. Yahya informed that Prince Muhammad being unable to face the royal army and escaped towards the Sirmur Hills.[17]

After the death of Sultan Ferozshah, Muhammad retreated from the Sirmur Hills and prepared to assert his claim to the throne. Delhi Sultan Ghiyasuddin deputed an army against his uncle Muhammad. Yahya writes about the compaign that when the Royal army entered the Sirmur Hills, the prince fled to Baknari Hill by an unknown track. The Royal army proceed ahead and give a flight in Baknari Valley. However, the Prince escaped without any harm and fled towards the Saket[18] through hills when the troops of royal army followed him. He went to Nagarkot. The royal soldiers pursued him upto Guler.[19] Prince Muhammad is reported to have consolidate his power in the fort against Delhi Sultan.[20]

From the above references it is clear that during the period under review Sirmur and its adjoining hills remained a hiding place for the rebels. The local chiefs like Rana Ranpal helped the rebels against Delhi Sultans. All the references indicates that the hills and forests of the Sirmur territory provided an easy shelter to the royal fugitives and rebels.

Sultan Balban was the first who invaded and plundered the Sirmur territory and capital. During the reign of Ferozshah Tughluq, Sirmur State and other Rais of hills remained loyal to Delhi. But after his death Sirmur again become a hinding shelter for royal fugitives like Prince Muhammad, Qatlug Khan, etc.

There is yet another important reference about the imperial attention being paid to this region during the rule of Sultan Ferozshah Tughluq. The Sultan completed one canal, *i.e.*, Firozabad canal staring from vicinity of Mandati and Sirmur Hills and uniting with other seven canals led to Hansi and then to Hisar Firoza.[21].

Nagarkot or Kangra

We find the references of Nagarkot in the persian sources as early in the period of Sultan Mahmud of Ghazni, Al-Utbi the contemporary chronicler of Sultan Mahmud refers to the Nagarkot in his work the *Kitab-ul-Yamini.*[22]

Utbi writes that Sultan Mahmud Ghazni took up the pursuit of the fugitives and followed them to the fort of Nagarkot which was situated near Kangra on the spur of a hill and was famous for wealth and held in great veneration. The Sultan interested in fort which fell after three days of heroic defence.[23]

According to both chroniclers Utbi and Gardizi, "Spoils beyond the limit of calculation, were captured by the conquerer. It consisted of 70,000,000 (crores) 'dirhams' of coined money, 70000 'Manns' of Gold and silver in got and costly apparel besides a folding house made of silver measuring 30×15 yards, a canopy of linen measuring 40×20 yards which was reared on poles of gold and silver."[24] Unsuri[25] enriched the reference that spoils also contains a richly decorated throne reputed to be that of Raja Bhim of the *Pandava dynasty*.[26]

Utbi writes that after the conquest of fort, Sultan Mahmud placed it in the charge of his officers and returned to Ghazni about to the end of the year 399 A.H./June, 1009 A.D.[27] The next reference to the Kangra is during the Prince Muhammad elder son of Sultan Gyasuddin Balban reign. Hazarat Amir Khusrau[28] writes in his *Diwan-Wast-ul-Hayat* that the Governor of Multan, Prince Sultan Muhammad deputed *Amir Hajib* Taqali and others to attach Nagarkot. The Rai of Nagarkot agreed to pay the *Jaziya*.[29]

The Badr-i-Chach also gives a reference regarding the conquest of Nagarkot by Sultan Muhammad-bin-Tughluq in A.H. 738/1337-38 A.D. He writes that Shahn Shah reached over this huge fort with one lack soldiers in the night. If he conquered the fort it would be in the name of the Caliph and if established a city it would be in the name of His servants.[30] Author of the *Sirat-i-Ferozshahi* writes that since the submission to Muhammad-bin-Tughluq in 1337 A.D. Kangra was governed by a Hindu Prince appointed by the Sultan of Delhi.[31]

Shamsu Siraj Afif in his, *Tarikh-i-Ferozshahi* records about the campaign and annexation of the Nagarkot. He narrates that Ferozshah personally led the army to Nagarkot to punish Rup Chand.[32] He besieged the fort by errecting "Manjaniks" and "Arradas". The arrival of the imperial army had alarmed the Rai who retired into the fortress leaving his country to the mercy of the invaders, who plundered it extensively.[33] The author of *Sirat-i-Ferozshahi* enrich the account with the reference that they opened the seize of fortress with beating of war drums and similar other instruments.[34]

The Raja of Nagarkot[35] exhibited unusual endurance and the seize lingered on for six months at the end of this the Rai submitted to the Sultan. Afif narrates a fanciful and incredible account of the manner of the Rai's submission. He writes that one day while Ferozshah was personally directing the seize operations. He noted that the Rai standing on the top of the fort stretching his hands in humility and submission. The Sultan in response to these submissive gestures of Rai waved his handkerchief and directed him to descent. Accordingly the Raja along with the member of his family and chiefs came down. The Rai offered valuable presents and submitted to the Sultan. The Sultan Feroz accepted the submission and patted the back of the Rai and also awarded him a robe and canopy besides many horses.[36]

The author of the *Sirat-i-Ferozshahi*, writes that Rai of Nagarkot was hard pressed by the seize. The Rai with his relatives sought forgiveness which the Sultan was gracious enough to accord.[37] The Kangra expedition of Ferozshah is also mentioned by a native chronicler, Manik Chand in his *Dharam Chand Natak*[38]. The Narrater mentions that Rup Chand went forth to meet the Sultan of Delhi and bowed very low down to feet. The Sultan put his hand on the Rup Chand's back.[39]

The persian chroniclers also narrates about the demolishing of Jawalamukhi temple.[40] After the submission of the Rai of Nagarkot Ferozshah intended to desecrate the idol and demolish the temple which also contained a huge collection of one thousand and three hundred books on various subjects. The Sultan marched to Jawala mukhi, all the books of the temple's library were captured to and later some of these on astronomy and other useful sciences were translated into persian verse. One of these books on rising and setting of the seven planets, their good and evil important omens was named by Izzuddin Khalid, *Dala'-it-i-Ferozshahi.*[41]

Other near contemporary Yahya or later chroniclers—Nizamuddin Ahmed and Abdur Qadir Badayuni do not confirm the demolition of the temple Jawalamukhi. But only Ferishta version that Sultan demolished the idol of Jawalamukhi.[42]

Afif narrates that after the capture of books sultan saw the idol and summoned the Rais, Zamindars, Rana and Brahmins of the place and addressed them, "Oh fools ! what is the use of praying to and worshiping this stone ? Our Holy Law tells us that those who oppose the decrees of our religion will go to hell." A rumour spread by Hindus that the sultan Ferozshah went to see the Jawalamukhi temple and presented a golden canopy to be hung over the idol. Afif added that this imputations against sultan was false and had been cancocted by the Hindus to slander and malign the Sultan who was a pious devotee, tree and God fearing Muslim and held the idol in deep destilation and subjected it to dignity.[43]

On the contrary the author of the *Sirat-i-Ferozshahi* nattates that when sultan marched to demolish the temple of Jawalamukhi. The Rana of Nagarkot requested Sultan Ferozshah that since he has submitted to His Majesty the order of demolition of the Temple, which was sacred to his subjects be withdrawn. He said that the late Sultan Muhammad-bin-Tughluq had also spared the Temple. Ferozshah in defence to and imitating his deceased patron withdraw the order.[44]

After the Tughluq's period we are unable to trace any reference Kangra during the Sayyad's period, however, during Sultan Sikandar Lodi's rule we find that sultan Sikandar Lodi ordered to conqueror the Hill terriories towards Nagarkot. Imperial soldiers conquered the hill states and demolished the temple. The army brought with them the idol of the temple which was given to the butchers to be weighed the flesh and canopy to the melted into pots.[45]

Therefore, it is clear from the forgoing accounts that in the majority of the eases the Sultans of Delhi invaded the Sirmur and Kangra to pursue and punish the rebels who had taken shelter with the local cheifs. However, the fugitives could not get any active help or co-operation from these hill cheiftains.

The cheif objective behind these expeditions were to punish the rebels rather than the subjugation or conquest of the Sirmur. But in case of Kangra's expeditions were motivated by the collection of tribute or establishing his suzerainty. Occassionally, the Sultans were successful in realising tribute or revenue from some of the cheifs as in case of Kangra. The chief was also oblized to pay *Jaziya* or tribute. However the Sultans of Delhi could not form a definite policy towards these Hill States and also fail to establish their sovereignty over the region.

REFERENCES

1. The erstwhile state of Sirmur lies along the outer Himalayan ranges between 75.5′ and 77.5′ East and 30.20′ and 31.5′ North. It is bounded on North by the Simla Hill States of Balasan and Jubbal, on East by the Tons River, on South it borders on the state of Kalsia and the Ambala Districts of United Punjab. *Sirmur State*, 1941, p. 1.

2. Nagarkot is a fort town situated on a hill which is presently known as Kangra. Kangra is one of the twelve districts of present Himachal Pradesh and lies between 31.20′ and 30.58′ North and 75.39′ and 78.35′ East. *Punjab District Gazetteer*, Vol. X-A, (Kangra District) part-A, (1904), p. 1 "Kot Kangra" stands over a lofty ridge south and above the town of Nagarkot. The fort is surrouded on three sides by inaccessible cliffs. *Imperial Gazetteer*, Vol.-XIV, p. 397. Literaly "Kangra" means a fortification of fortrees. It occupies long narrow strip of land on the fort between Manjhi and Banganga rivers. Its wall are upwards two miles in circut but its strength does not lies in its wall but in its precipitions over hanging the rivers. A. Cunnigham, *Arechaeological Survey Reports*, Vol. v, pp. 162-63. The rulers of Kangra belonged to the Katoch dynasty—*Punjab Gazetteer*, Vol. 1, p. 355. First Historical figure of the dynasty was Susar man Chandra the 234 from founders. He built the second capital of his state at Nagarkot after the close of the Mahabharat (First capital was Jalandhar). After the Mohammedan invasions the territories on the plain lest and Nagarkot became the cheif capital of Katoch—J. Hutchision and J.Ph. Vogel, "History of *Kangra* State", Pub. in the *Journal of Punjab Historical Society*, 1920,

Vol.-vii, pp. 12-21, This fort also known as the fort of Bhim.

3. During the reign of Sultan Rajiya (1237-49 A.D.) Wazir Nizamulmulk Junaidi, (along with his associates Iqtadars of Multan, Hansi, Lahore and Buda'un) declined to recognise the Sultans suzerainty. Sultan Rajiya was unable to give a battle and turned her proximity to their camp to gained account and consequently Junaidi lost the faith of his associates.

4. Mihaj Siraj, *Tabaqat-i-Nasiri*, Calcutta text, pp. 186-87, S.A.A. Rizvi, *Adi Turk Kalin Bharat*, Aligarh, 1956, p. 34, Minhaj further remarks that he also died there.

5. *Ibid.*, p 292.

6. Qatlugh Khan has married the Sultan's mother. Sultan ordered him to go to Awadh where he attempt to organise the anti-Turkish force but as soon as Balban reassumed his office he marched against him and defeated. In A.H. 654/1256 A.D. Qatlugh Khan succeeded in occuping Awadh and even attempted to capture Kara and Manikpur but was defeated.

7. Minhaj, *Ibid.*, p. 221.

8. *Ibid.*, p. 222.

9. *Ibid.*, pp. 306-7.

10. *Ibid.*, pp. 306-7.

11. Yahya-bin-Ahmed Sirhindi completed *Tarikh-i-Mubarakshahi* in 1434 A.D.

12. Yahya, *Tarikh-i-Mubarakshahi*, Calcutta text, p. 73, S.A.A. Rizvi, *Khalji Kalin Bharat*, Aligarh, 1955, p. 222.

13. A.H. 5 Safar, 763/Friday, 23 March 1352 A.D.

14. *Ibid.*, p. 123, Nizamuddin Ahmed, *Tabaqat-i-Akbari*, Calcutta text, p. 228, it also confirm this fact by Ferishta, *Tarikh-i-Ferishta*, Vol. 1, p. 146.

15. *Ibid.*, p. 134, *Yahya*, Basu text, p. 141, *Sirmur State Gezetteer*, p. 1, Nizamuddin also confirm this event, *op. cit.*, p. 235.

16. *Ibid.*, p. 138, N. Ajmed, *op. cit.*, p. 237.

17. *Ibid.*, p. 139, *Yahya*, Basu text, pp. 144-45.

18. "Saket is an old name of the Sundernagar constituency of District Mandi (H.P.).

19. For detail see—*Ibid.*, p. 142, N. Ahmed, *op. cit.*, p. 242.

20. *Ibid.*, p. 145, *Ibid.*, p. 243.

21. *Ibid*,. p. 125, *Yahya*, Basu text, pp. 130-31, Anonymous, *Sirat-i-Ferozshahi*, Patna MSS., pp. 154-55.

22. It covers the period of Subukatgin and Sultan Mahmud upto A.H. 411/1020 A.D. The style of writing is very ornate and verbose.

23. Al-Utbi, *Kitab-ul-Yamini*, Lahore, 1300 A.H., pp, 224-26, Gardizi, *Zain'ul-Akhbar*, ed. by M.Nazim, p. 70.

24. *Ibid.*, p. 226.

25. Unsuri's *Diwan*, is also an important source. He was a poet. His qasidas in the Sultan Mahmud contains many Historical facts which are useful in correcting and supplementing the accounts of the contemporary historians.

26. Unsuri *Diwan*, (ed. Tehram, n.d.), p. 85.

27. *Al-Utbi*, *op. cit.*, p. 226. According to Gardizi, *op. cit.*, p. 70., the Sultan ordered that spoils to be displayed in public in the begining of A.H. 400/August/September, 1009 A.D.

28. Amir Khusrau writes historical facts in verse. His refereces to the Medieval Himachal History are however, worthy of credence. Most of the Historians did not utilize the material even up to the present time.

29. For detail see—A. Khusrau, *Diwan-wast, ul-hayat*, Aligarh, n.d., Stanzas 86-145.

30. Badr-i-Chach, *Qasida-i-Badri-i-Chach*, Newal Kishor Press, 1873, pp. 28-29.

31. Anonymous, *Sirat-i-Ferozshahi*, *op. cit.*, p. 73.

32. Ferishta records an accident which throws light on his conduct, that the Raja of Nagarkot come out with his army on a raiding expeditions and plundered the plains upto Delhi while he was returning with loaded war booty. His army encountered by Sultan Shahbuddin of Kashmir near Satluj and was defeated. He surrendered all the spils to Kashmiri Sultan and swore fealthy to him. For detail see—Ferishta, *op. cit.*, Vol. I, p. 458-59, Jon Raj's, *Raj Taranginni*, (eng. tr.), Vol. III, p. 39, also refers this incident.

33. Afif, *Tarih-i-Ferozshahi*, Calcutta text, pp. 186-90.

34. Sirat, *op. cit.*, p. 74.

35. The name of the ruler has been mentioned as Shastra Chandra.

36. Afif, *op. cit.*, pp. 188-89, Bihamad Khani Mohammad, *Tarikh-i-Mohammadi*, (Br. Mus. MS), ff. 410 a, b.

37. Sirat, *op. cit.*, pp. 74, N. Ahmad, *op. cit.*, p. 233.

38. There is written in 1563 A.D., auther was a native political chronicler.

39. Manik Chand writes in these words :

    'Rup Chander Barkar Dilashwar Sultan,
    Bahut Helkar Pag Dharo Pith Hath le San'

40. "The ancient site of Dehra Gopipur, a Tesil of Kangra District situated on the road from Kangra town to Nadaon at the foot of precipitious range of Hills. It is famous for the temple of Goddess Jawalamukhi. She is of the flaming mouth". A Cummigham, *op. cit.*, Vol. V, pp. 169-70, *Punjab Gazetteer*, Vol. I, p. 387.

41. N. Ahmad, *op. cit.*, p. 234.

42. Ferishta writes that the Sultan broke the idol of Jawalamukhi mixed its fragments with the flesh of cows and hanged them in the bags around the neck of Brahmins who were paraded through the camp and sent the principal idol as a trouphy to Madina-Ferishta, *op. cit.*, Vol. I, p. 454.

43. Afif, *op. cit.*, pp. 186-87.

44. Sirat, p. 76.

45. Abdullah, *Tarikh-i-Davali* (Aligarh 1952), p. 37.

APPENDIX

LIST OF THE QAZIAN DURING DELHI SULTANATE
(1206-1526 A.D.)

S. No.	Rank	Name	Place	Period
(1)	(2)	(3)	(4)	(5)
		(A) *Sultan Qutbuddin Aibaq* (*1206-10 A.D.*)		
1.	Qazi-ul-Quazat	Kamaluddin Muhammad	Hind & Sindh	—
2.	Qazi-i-Mamalik	Sharful Mulk	Delhi	—
3.	Qazi-ul-Quzat	Wazhuddin Kashani	—	—
4.	Qazi	Sharafuddin	Multan	—

(Contd.)

(*Contd.*)

(1)	(2)	(3)	(4)	(5)
		(B) *Sultan Shamsuddin Iltutmish (1210-35 A.D.)*		
5.	Qazi-i-Lashkar	Kabiruddin	—	—
6.	,,	Minhaj Siraj	Alauddin Masud's army	1227-28 A.D.
7.	,,	,,	Royal Army	1228-32 A.D.
8.	Qazi-ul-Quzat	Wazihuddin Kashani	Delhi	—
9.	Qaza, Khitabat, Ahtisab	Minhaj Siraj	Gwalior	1232-35 A.D.
10.	Qazi	Hamiduddin Nagori	Delhi	—
11.	,,	Hussain	—	—
12.	,,	Hasan	—	—
13.	,,	Imad	—	—
14.	,,	Jalaluddin	—	—
15.	,,	Jalaluddin Ghazanabi	—	—
16.	,,	Nasiruddin Kasli	—	—
17.	,,	Nizam	—	—
18.	,,	Qutabuddin Kashani	—	—
19.	,,	Sad	—	—

20.	,,	Saduddin Karori	—	—
21.	,,	Sayyid	—	—
22.	,,	Sayyiduddin Gardezi	—	—
		(C) *Sultan Rukanuddin Ferozshah (1235-36 A.D.)*		
23.	Qazi	Hamiduddin Nagori	Nagore	1235-36 A.D.
		(D) *Sultan Raziya (1236-41 A.D.)*		
24.	Qazi	Hamiduddin	Nagore	1236-40 A.D.
25.	,,	Minhaj Siraj	Gawalior	1238-41 A.D.
26.	,,	Nasiruddin	—	—
		(E) *Sultan Muizuddin Bahram Shah (1241-42 A.D)*		
27.	Qazi-i-Mamalik	Jalaluddin Kashani	Delhi	1241-42 A.D.
28.	Qaza	Minhaj Siraj	Delhi	1241-42 A.D.
29.	Qazi	Hamiduddin	Nagore	—
30.	,,	Kabiruddin	Delhi	—
31.	,,	Shamsuddin Mihri	Mihrpur	–
		(F) *Sultan Alauddin Masud Shah (1242-46 A.D.)*		
32.	Qazi-ul-Quzat	Imaduddin Muhammad Shafukani	Delhi	1242-45 A.D.
33.	,,	Jalaluddin Kashani	,,	1245 46 A.D.

(Contd-)

(*Contd.*)

(1)	(2)	(3)	(4)	(5)
34.	Qaza	Minhaj Siraj	Gwalior	1245-46 A.D.
35.	Qazi	Hamiduddin Nagori	Nagore	—
36.	,,	Jalaluddin Kashani	Awadh	1242-45 A.D.
37.	,,	Jalaluddin Kashani	Delhi	1246-47 A.D.
38.	,,	Jalaluddin Lawrenji	—	—
39.	,,	Jalaluddin Lawrenji	Awadh	—
40.	,,	Muhiuddin Kashani	—	—
		(G) *Sultan Nasiruddin Mahmud (1246-66 A.D.)*		
41.	Qazi-i-Mamalik	Imaduddin Shafurkani	Delhi	1246-49 A.D.
42.	,,	Jalaluddin Kashani	,,	1249-51 A.D.
43.	,,	Minhaj Siraj	,,	1251-53 A.D.
44.	,,	,,	,,	1255 A.D to till Death
45.	,,	Shamsuddin Baihraichi	,,	1253-55 A.D.
46.	Qazi, Sheikh-ul-Islam	Qutabuddin	Delhi	—

47.	Qazi	Imam Hamiduddin Magrila	—	Till death (1259 A.D.)
48.	,,	Unknown (Son of the former Qazi)	—	1259-unknown A.D.
49.	,,	Imad Khan	—	—
50.	,,	Imaduddin Shafurkani	Ranthumbhor	—
51.	,,	Kabiruddin	—	Till death (1259 A.D.)
52.	,,	Unknown (Son of former Qazi)	—	1259-unknown A.D.
53.	,,	Kamaluddin Jafri	Badaun	—
54.	,,	Shamsuddin Baihraichi	,,	—
		(H) *Sultan Gyasuddin Balban (1266-86 A.D.)*		
55.	Qazi, Sadr-i-Jahan	Fakhruddin Naqila	Delhi	1266-86 A.D.
56.	Qazi-i-Lashkar	Sadiduddin	—	—
57.	Qazi	Asiruddin Muhammad	Delhi	—
58.	,,	Fakhruddin	—	—
59.	,,	Jahiruddin	—	—
60.	,,	Jalaluddin	—	—

(Contd.)

(*Contd.*)

(1)	(2)	(3)	(4)	(5)
61.	,,	Jalaluddin Kashani	Delhi	—
62.	,,	Qutab Kashani	—	—
63.	Qazi	Rafi'uddin Gazruni	—	—
64.	,,	Rukanuddin Samana	Samana	—
65.	,,	Shamsuddin Maraji	—	—
66.	,,	Sharafuddin Balhaqi	—	—
67.	,,	Tahiruddin	—	—
		(I) *Sultan Muizzuddin Quiqubad (1286-88 A.D.)*		
68.	Qazi-ul-Quzat	Malik Nizamuddin	Delhi	—
69.	Qazi, Sadr-i-Jahan	Jalaluddin Kashani	—	—
70.	Qazi	Alam	—	—
71.	,,	Mihri (not clear)	Mihrpur	—
72.	,,	Sharfuddin Surpa	—	—
		(J) *Sultan Jalaluddin Ferozshah Khalji (1290-96 A.D.)*		
73.	Qazi, Sadr-i-Jahan	Ziauddin Savi	Delhi	—

74.	Qazi-i-Lashkar	Ziauddin Bayanavi	Bayana	—
75.	Qazi	Alam Diwana	Delhi	—
76.	,,	Amad	—	—
77.	,,	Ainuddin	—	—
78.	,,	Bana'i Suqi	—	—
79.	,,	Burhanuddin	—	—
80.	,,	Fakhruddin Naqila	—	—
81.	,,	Imaduddin Raji	—	—
82.	,,	Jalaluddin Kashani	Delhi	—
83.	,,	Kamaluddin	Badaun	—
84.	,,	Khalid	—	—
85.	,,	Madud	—	—
86.	,,	Mughisuddin	Bayana	Whole region
87.	,,	Raziuddin	—	—
88.	,,	Sadr Muhammad Yusuf	—	—
89.	,,	Sadruddin A'rif	Kara	—
90.	,,	Shamsuddin	—	—
91.	,,	Wahiduddin	—	—

(*Contd.*)

(Contd.)

(1)	(2)	(3)	(4)	(5)
92.	,,	Yaqub	—	—
93.	,,	Zahiruddin	—	—
		(K) *Sultan Alauddin Muhammad Khalji (1296-1316 A.D.)*		
94.	Qazi-i-Mamalik	Hamiduddin	Delhi	1296-1316 A.D.
95.	Sadr-i-Jahan, Qazi-i-Mamalik	Sadruddin A'rif	—	—
96.	Qazi-i-Lashkar	Ziauddin Bayana	Court of Delhi	—
97.	Qaza	Hamiduddin Multani	Multan	—
98.	Naib-i-Qaza	Jalaluddin Balbalji	Bayana	—
99.	Qazi-Khan	Ziauddin	Delhi	1296-1316 A.D.
100.	Naib-i-Qazi	Sadruddin A'rif	—	—
101.	Qazi	Fakhruddin Naqila	—	—
102.	,,	Hamiduddin	Bayana	—
103.	,,	Mughisuddin Bayanwi	—	—
104.	,,	Muhiddin Kashani	—	—
105.	,,	Maulana Murshid Kuhrami	Court of Sultan	1296-1316 A.D.
106.	,,	Maulana Zahir	—	—

107.	,,	Shamsuddin Gazaruni	—	—
108.	,,	Sharfuddin Sarbahi	—	—
109.	,,	Sayyid Ruqanuddin	Kara	—
110.	,,	Sayyid Tajuddin	Badaun	—
111.	,,	Zainuddin Naqila	—	—
		(L) *Sulton Qutabuddin Mubarak Shah Khalji* (*1316-19 A.D.*)		
112.	Sadr-i-Jahan Qazi Khan	Ziauddin	Delhi	1316-19 A.D.
113.	Qazi	Zan'uddin Mubarak	Gawalior (Fort)	—
		(M) *Sultan Ghiyasuddin Tughluq* (*1320-25 A.D*)		
114.	Sadr-i-Jahan, Qazi-i-Mamalik	Kamaluddin	Delhi	1320-25 A.D.
115.	Qazi, Naib-i-Hakim	Jalaluddin Karenzi	—	—
116.	Qazi	Hamiduddin Nagori	Nagore	—
117.	,,	S'alar	Multan	—
118.	,,	Shamsuddin (Shama'uddin)	Delhi	—
		(N) *Sultan Muhammad-Bin-Tughluq* (*1325-51 A.D.*)		
119.	Qazi-ul-Quzat Mamalik	Kamaluddin Gazanawi	Delhi	—
120.	Qazi-ul-Qazat, Sadr-i-Jahan	Nasiruddin Nasurzi	,,	—

(Contd.)

Contd.)

(1)	(2)	(3)	(4)	(5)
121.	,,	Sharf Jahan	Daultabad	—
122.	Qazi Imam	Imam Shamnuddin	Chanderi	—
123.	Qazi	Ibn-i-Batutta	Delhi	1333-42 A.D.
124.	,,	Jalal	Baroda	—
125.	,,	Jalal Afghan	Koel	—
126.	,,	Kashna	Gazni	—
127.	,,	Majduddin	—	—
128.	,,	Malik-Sharif Jalaluddin	Uchch	—
129.	,,	Mazduddin Siraj	—	—
130.	,,	Nizamuddin Yahya	Multan	—
131.	,,	Nur'uddin	Hinaur	—
132.	,,	Qazi Khasa	Chanderi	—
133.	,,	Qiwamuddin	Tirmiz	—
134.	,,	Sadruddin Hanifi'	Bhakkar	—
135.	,,	Saifuddin	Argah	—
136.	,,	Sa'lar	Multan	—

137.	Qazi	Sharafuddin	—	—
138.	,,	Shrif Amir Ali	Amroha	—
139.	,,	Wajihulmulk	Daultabad	—
140.	,,	Zainuddin	—	—
		(O) *Sultan Ferozshah Tughluq 1351-88 A.D.)*		
141.	Qazi, Sadr-i-Jahan	Sayyid Jalaluddin Kirmani	Delhi	—
142.	Qazi-i-Lashkar	Nasr'ullah	Sultan's Army	—
143.	Qazi-i-Shah	Malik Burhanuddin	Sultan's Court	—
144.	Qazi	A'bid	—	—
145.	,,	Bagdadichajju	—	—
146.	,,	Husamuddin	—	—
147.	,,	Malik Abdullah	—	—
148.	,,	Misr	—	—
149.	,,	Sadrumulk	Mahoba	—
150.	,,	Sharf	Somnath	—
151.	,,	Shihabuddin Daultabadi	Daultabad	—
		(P) *Sultanate of Saiyyids and Lodis (1414-1526 A.D.)*		
152.	Qazi, Hajib	Wahid	Thaneshwar	—
153.	Qazi	Abdul Khair	—	—

(Contd.)

(*Contd.*)

(1)	(2)	(3)	(4)	(5)
154.	,,	Abdullah	Ajudhan	—
155.	,,	Abdullah	Thaneshwar	—
156.	,,	Abdul Wahab	Kabul	—
157.	,,	Abdur Rehman	—	—
158.	,,	Abu Yusuf	Malwa	—
159.	,,	Amanad	Broda	—
160.	,,	Badruddin Mabri	Mabar	—
161.	,,	Chaq	Kashmir	1488-1517 A.D.
162.	,,	Fatalu'llah	—	—
163.	,,	Husamuddin	Gujarat	—
164.	,,	Junaid	—	—
165.	,,	Kamaluddin Jafri	Badaun	—
166.	,,	Mian Bhury	—	—
167.	,,	Mian Qa'dan	Delhi	—
168.	,,	Muhammad	Multan	—
169.	,,	Nasiruddiu Kasa	—	—

170.	,,	Nizamuddin	—	—
171.	,,	Pir Ishaq	Sultanpur	Sultanpur
172.	,,	Piyara'	Lakhnur	1488-1517 A.D.
173.	,,	Qazan	Sind	—
174.	,,	Qutabpir	—	—
175.	,,	Sha Khu	Daccen	—
176.	,,	Sheikh Budh	Lakhnur	—
177.	,,	Sheikh Jamaluddin Sulaimani	Kahtwal	—
178.	,,	Shihabuddin	Jaunpur	—
179.	,,	Shihabuddin Jaunpuri	Bengal	—
180	,,	Shuaib	Kahtwal	—
181.	,,	Unknown	Sonkhera	—

Thus, we are able to conclude the numbers of the different ranks of Qazian during the Delhi Sultanate such as :

1.	"Naib-i-Qaza"	1
2.	"Naib-i-Qazi"	1
3.	"Qaza"	3
4.	"Qazi-Iman"	1
5.	"Qazi-Khan"	1
6.	"Qazi-i-Lashkar"	/
7.	"Qazi-i-Mamalik"	8
8.	"Qazi Sadr-i-Jahan"	5

9.	"Qazi-i-Shah"	1
10.	"Qazi-Naib-i-Hakim"	1
11.	"Qazi, Sheikh-ul-Islam"	1
12.	"Qazi-ul-Quzat"	6
13.	"Qazi-ul-Quzat-Mamalik"	1
14.	"Qazi-ul-Quzat, Sadr-i-Jahan"	2
15.	"Sadr-i-Jahan, Qazi-i-Mamalik"	2
16.	"Qazi"	141
	TOTAL :	182

This shows that jurisdiction and powers of Qazi were limited or un-limited according to their appointment letter.

S. No. 48 and 52 shows that office of "Qaza" may be attained the hereditory nature. Similarly the office of "Qaza" was continuely influenced by the contemporary political unheavels such as every new sultan has appointed a new Qazi in the office of "Qaza".

Index